TEACHING 1, 2, 3 JOHN

From text to message

MERVYN ELOFF

SERIES EDITORS: DAVID JACKMAN & ADRIAN REYNOLDS

TEACHING
1, 2, 3 JOHN

From text to message

MERVYN ELOFF

SERIES EDITORS: DAVID JACKMAN & ADRIAN REYNOLDS

PT RESOURCES
CHRISTIAN
FOCUS

ISBN 978-1-78191-832-6

10 9 8 7 6 5 4 3 2 1

Published in 2016
by
Christian Focus Publications Ltd,
Geanies House, Fearn, Ross-shire,
IV20 1TW, Scotland, Great Britain
with
Proclamation Trust Resources,
Willcox House, 140-148 Borough High Street,
London, SE1 1LB, England, Great Britain.
www.proctrust.org.uk

www.christianfocus.com

Cover design by Moose77.com

Printed and bound by Nørhaven, Denmark

Contents

Author's Preface

My first encounter with John's letters came when still a relatively new believer. I had heard and believed the glorious gospel of God's grace in Jesus Christ and I certainly knew that my sins had been forgiven and that I had been given the gift of eternal life. But as time went by the reality of my ongoing sinfulness began to threaten my assurance of salvation. How could I claim to be a Christian and yet fail in so many different ways? A good friend and wise pastor pointed me to 1 John and, though I did not fully understand everything, I learned two very important lessons. First, I learned that there is a connection between sin and assurance and that only a robust understanding of the death of Jesus for sinners can enable a sinner to live with certainty. In the words of 1 John 3:20, I learned that 'God is greater than our hearts'. Secondly, I learned that true assurance is not mere affirmation but a reality rooted in objective evidence and mediated through the work of God's Holy Spirit. And as I examined my own life in the light of John's so-called 'tests' or perhaps better 'evidences' of authentic Christian experience, I found myself assured but also challenged to hold fast to the truth, to walk in the light and to walk in love. Thus 1 John taught me that authentic assurance is not arrogant presumption but humble, confident, grateful perseverance.

As a pastor, I have come to see that the question of assurance is one of those perennial questions that Christians face, sometimes even after many years of walking with the Lord. Sometimes the issue is one of temperament, sometimes doubts arise in the face of difficult circumstances or in the light of some besetting sin. Often, however, doubts arise in the face of some 'new teaching' and the confident claims for a superior spirituality that the proponents and followers of this teaching make. Foundational doctrines are treated with disdain and dismissed as no longer relevant or indeed appropriate in a more enlightened age; new perspectives on faith and practice are brought to the fore and advocated as the way ahead for a church seeking to stay in touch with the world around it. And all the while, assurances are given that the new way is the better way and that God is pleased that the church is finally coming of age!

Thankfully, of course, there are many believers who see through these claims and who stay true to what has been taught 'from the beginning'. But there are those whose zeal outstrips their knowledge, who have their heads turned by the new teaching and who, as a result, are drawn away. And within this unsettled and divisive environment there are always those who are plunged into confusion and whose confidence in their own relationship with the Lord is severely shaken. It was for such as these that John's letters were written, countering the boastful claims of the new teachers, calling the church back to its historic faith and way of life and, in this way, providing a firm and assured foundation for authentic fellowship with God .

I am deeply grateful for the congregation of St James Church, Kenilworth among whom it has been my very great pleasure and privilege to serve and, in recent times, to study John's letters. Week by week, as we wrestled together with the text, I have been encouraged and edified by their wholehearted commitment both to hear and to do the Word of God. I am more indebted than I can say to Frank Retief, the good friend and wise pastor, who led me to the Lord and pointed me to 1 John in my times of doubt, and to Dick Lucas who has been a constant encouragement to me and a magnificent example of an authentic and unashamed workman, one who rightly handles the Word of Truth. I know that I speak for many as I thank him for his ministry. My thanks also go to the Proclamation Trust for the opportunity to write this book and to Adrian Reynolds and David Jackman for their editorial work.

Last, but by no means least, my thanks to 'my girls' – my beloved wife Alison and daughters Kirstin and Rebecca who are for me a great treasure and a constant source of joy and encouragement.

As we study and teach John's letters, may the God who is light and love grant that we, together with His people, may know both joy and deep assurance as we walk by faith and in fellowship with Him.

Mervyn Eloff
Cape Town
2016

Series Preface

The letters of John, which we know by their numbers (1, 2 and 3 John) are among the least preached of the New Testament letters. The density of the language, the apparent repetition of key ideas (although, as we shall see, this is a mis-reading of the text), the difficult ideas – all of these contribute to the preacher or teachers' hesitation in visiting this unfamiliar territory. That is not to say that there are not familiar texts and purple passages. Some of the New Testament's most 'famous' texts can be found here. However, as entire letters, they are often overlooked and that is why *Teaching John's Letters* is such an important contribution to our series. We need help getting the familiar parts right and tackling the denser sections carefully. Mervyn's volume does both of these things superbly well.

The volumes are purposely practical, seeking to offer real help for those involved in teaching the Bible to others. The preacher or teacher, the sermon or talk, and the listener are the key 'drivers' in this series. The Introductory Section contains basic 'navigation' material to get you into the text of the letters, covering aspects like structure and planning a preaching series. The 'meat' of the book then works systematically through the major sections, suggesting preaching or teaching units, including sermon outlines and questions for Bible studies. These are not there to take the hard work out of preparation, but as a starting point to get you thinking about how to preach the material or prepare a Bible study.

Teaching John's Letters brings the number of published volumes in the series to [16]. We are encouraged at how the series is developing and the positive comments from the people that really matter – those at the chalk face of Christian ministry, working hard at the word, week in week out, to proclaim the unsearchable riches of Christ.

Our thanks must go to Celia Reynolds and Jaz Rebera for help with proofreading, checking references and making amendments. As ever, our warm gratitude goes to the team at Christian Focus for their committed partnership in this project.

David Jackman &
Adrian Reynolds
Series Editors
London 2016

How to use this Book

This book aims to help the preacher or teacher understand the central aim and purpose of the text, in order to preach or teach it to others. Unlike a commentary, therefore, it does not go into great exegetical detail. Instead it helps us to engage with the themes of John's letters, to keep the big picture in mind, and to think about how to present it to our hearers.

'Part One: Introducing John's Letters' examines the three books' themes and structure. This material is crucial to our understanding of the letters, which will shape the way we preach each section to our congregations. As a preliminary to the rest of the book, it divides the Bible books up into manageable units. The remainder of the volume contains separate chapters on each preaching unit considered in Part One. The structure of each chapter is the same: it begins with a brief introduction to the unit followed by a section headed 'Listening to the text.' This section outlines the structure and context of the unit and takes the reader through a section by section analysis of the text. All good biblical preaching begins with careful, detailed listening to the text and this is true for New Testament letters as much as any other genre of the Word of God.

Each chapter then continues with a section called 'From text to message.' This suggests a main theme and aim for each preaching unit (including how the unit relates to the overall theme of the book) and then some possible sermon outlines. These suggestions are nothing more than that – suggestions designed to help the preacher think about his own division of the text and the structure of the sermon. We are great believers in every preacher constructing his own outlines, because they need to flow from our personal encounter with God in the text. Downloading other people's sermons or trying to breathe life into someone else's outlines are strategies doomed to failure. They may produce a reasonable talk, but in the long term, they are disastrous to the preacher himself since he needs to live in the word and the word to live in him, if he is to speak from the heart of God to the hearts of his congregation. These sections are deliberately brief, therefore. However, especially for those just starting out, it can be helpful to see how a sermon might shape up.

Each chapter concludes with some suggested questions for a group Bible study split into two types: questions to help *understand* the passage and questions to help *apply* the passage. Not all the questions would be needed for a study, but they give some ideas for those who are planning a study series. The aim of good questions is always to drive the group into the text, to explore and understand its meaning more fully. This keeps the focus on Scripture and reduces speculation and the mere exchange of opinions. Remember the key issues are always, 'What does the text say?' and then 'What does it mean'? Avoid the 'What does it mean to you?' type of question. It is much better to discuss the application more generally and personally after everyone understands the intended meaning, so that the Bible really is in the driving-seat of the study, not the participants' opinions, prejudices or experiences! These studies will be especially useful in those churches where Bible study groups are able to study the book at the same time as it is preached, a practice we warmly commend. This allows small groups to drive home understanding, and especially application, in the week after the sermon has been preached, ensuring it is applied to the daily lives of the congregation.

Part I
Introducing John's Letters

I

Getting our Bearings in John's Letters

Introduction

Let me begin with a rather cheeky question: Why bother to read this Introduction? Given the time pressure we all face, should one not pass over the preliminaries and 'plunge straight in' with exegesis of the text? Of course careful exegesis is the essential work of the Bible teacher, the key building block of a proper framework of understanding of the text and the book as a whole. But there is surely also real value in having at least some preliminary understanding of the overall shape of the book and its key concerns, of having a 'starter' framework which our exegetical work can then shape and modify. This Introduction is thus designed not to have the last word but to provide just such a 'starter' framework, a solid foundation for the exegetical work that follows.

When and by whom were the letters written?

Given the formal anonymity of the letters we know as 1, 2 and 3 John, it is hardly surprising that there has been a great deal of debate and disagreement about the authorship of these letters, their date of composition and the particular setting which gave rise to them. The present designation of these letters as 1, 2 and 3 John reflects an ancient and venerable tradition that these three letters are the work of the author of the Fourth Gospel, John the beloved disciple and apostle of the Lord Jesus. The claim by the author in the opening verses of 1 John to eye- and ear-witness authority certainly points in that direction and even the author's self-designation as 'the elder' in 2 and 3 John, though unusual, does not, in this view, detract from Johannine authorship any more than Peter's description of himself as a 'fellow elder' in 1 Peter 5:1 negates his own apostolic authority. Indeed, the term may have been used by the author in 2 and 3 John to highlight the particularly close relationship which he enjoyed with the specific congregations to which these letters are addressed in distinction to the more general, though still authoritative, relationship which he had with the wider church.

The majority view is that the letters share a common authorship and that the links with the Fourth Gospel are very strong, though for some this fact is simply an indication of the influence of the Fourth Gospel within the community rather than a result of common authorship. There is far less agreement regarding the identity of the author, with many, though by no means all, in more recent times, preferring to ascribe the work to an unknown member or members of the so-called Johannine School or Community. The evidence, both *pro* and *con*, can be found in the introductory material of the standard commentaries and reference works and need not detain us here. Speaking personally, there seems to be no good reason to reject the traditional view that the

Apostle John was responsible for the letters and that they were thus in all likelihood written toward the end of the first century and set in or around Ephesus.

Why were the letters written?

If, as Colin Kruse rightly reminds us, we are 'careful' and 'judicious' in reading and especially in reading between the lines of the text of 1, 2 and 3 John, we can, in fact, discover a good deal about the situation that gave rise to these letters and the author's purpose in writing them. The clearest statement of purpose is, of course, found in 1 John 5:13 where the author himself declares that he wrote so that those 'who believe in the name of the Son of God...may know that (they) (*lit* you) have eternal life.' But, as Matthew Jensen points out in his excellent and thought-provoking article on the structure and argument of 1 John, this is by no means the only reference to the author's activity of writing in the letter. The verb 'write' and its cognates in fact occur thirteen times in 1 John, sometimes to designate a particular group (e.g. 1 John 2:12-14), sometimes to give a reason for writing (1 John 2:1), sometimes to reinforce some aspect of what has been taught (1 John 2:7-8). On two occasions, however (1 John 1:4; 1 John 5:13), the verb is used to describe the author's specific purpose in writing the letter as a whole. As we shall see in our detailed discussion of the text, in 1 John 1:4 we are told that the purpose in writing was to promote authentic and joyful fellowship with the Father, a fellowship which the author and his associates themselves enjoy and which is characterised 'walking in the light' (1 John 1:7). As already noted above, we are told in 1 John 5:13 that the purpose in writing was to establish true assurance for believers in Jesus.

On closer examination of 1 John, however, we discover that this concern for the readers' joyful and assured fellowship with God is prompted by the spurious and deeply unsettling claims of a group of teachers who, having been part of the community, have now withdrawn (1 John 2:19), but whose influence nevertheless remains a threat (1 John 2:26). It seems reasonable to assume that it is this group of 'secessionists', who are in view in 2 John 7-11 and that the purpose of 2 John was, among other things, to ensure that these false teachers who had 'gone out into the world' (2 John 7) were not given a hearing within the local churches, lest they turn their hearers away from 'the teaching of Christ' (2 John 9). By contrast, in 3 John the elder is writing to encourage both Gaius and the church to which he belonged to welcome and support those who 'went out for the sake of the Name' (3 John 7 NASB). As we shall see, both 2 and 3 John underline the fact that truth and love are inseparable and thus serve to encourage believers to keep walking in both truth and love.

In summary then, we can say that John's letters were written to assure true believers in Jesus in their relationship with the Lord and to encourage them to keep walking in the truth and in love so that they may continue to enjoy fellowship with God. To this end the letters proclaim the way of truth and love as it is found in Jesus the Christ and warn against the teaching of those who, though they claim great things, are in fact enemies of the truth. Precisely what these claims are and how they are answered in the letters will be seen in the detailed discussion of the text.

How are the letters structured?

Given the presence of traditional formulae, namely *address – greeting – main content – concluding greetings*, 2 and 3 John are both clearly identifiable as typical Greco-Roman letters. Their brevity also means that an analysis of the structure of each letter is quite straightforward. The letters can be subdivided as follows:

2 John

vv. 1-3	Opening greeting stressing the link between love and truth
vv. 4-6	Encouragement to walk in both truth and love
vv. 7-11	Warning against those who do not walk in the truth. Because truth and love are linked, don't welcome or assist those who don't teach the truth
vv. 12-13	Final greetings. A reminder of the reality and joy of fellowship in the truth

3 John

v. 1	Opening greeting stressing the link between love and truth
vv. 2-12	Truth and love in practice: A contrast between Diotrephes and Demetrius
vv. 13-14	Final greetings. A reminder of the reality and joy of fellowship in the truth

When it comes to 1 John, however, the question about structure is not so easily answered. A number of different approaches have been proposed based variously on content, theme, grammar, literary form or a combination of the above. An evaluation of the suggested structural analyses, though time consuming and sometimes frustrating, is however a worthwhile exercise, not so much for the conclusions reached as for the discipline of a careful, repeated reading of the text as a whole. It is as we grapple with the text over and over again, noting not only what it says but how it says what it says, that we begin to develop a feel for the author's key beliefs and primary concerns and therefore for the meaning and application of the text.

Worth noting in particular in 1 John are:-

- The numerous references to *writing* (see above) indicating either the author's purpose and reason for writing or of the content of the letter.

- The repeated use of the word *proclaim* (1:1,2,3) and the references to the *message heard and declared* (1:5; 2:7; 3:11) standing in stark contrast to the *claims* and *statements* made by the so-called enlightened teachers (1:6,8,10; 2:4,6,9; 4:20). Also noteworthy in this connection are the repeated phrases 'this is the message' (1:5; 3:11) and 'from the beginning' (1:1; 2:7,13,14,24; 3:8,11).

- The twin theological declaration 'God is light' (1:5) and 'God is love' (4:8,16) which is also very striking when read in conjunction with the letter's final verse: 'Dear children, keep yourself from idols' (5:21). This two-fold declaration about God, together with the phrase 'this is the message', is taken by some e.g. Brown to suggest a two-fold division for the letter, the first half (1:5–3:10) focussing on the theological and moral implications of God being light; the second (3:11–5:12) focussing on the theological and moral implications of God being love. To this two-part division are then added a prologue (1:1-4) and epilogue (5:15-21).

- The bracketing or 'sandwich' based on the words *light* and *darkness* (1:5–2:11) and the repetition of the word *world* in 2:15–5:12. Also noteworthy here are the clusters of verses in which the words 'sin' (1:6–2:2; 3:4-9; 5:16-18) and 'love' (2:3-11; 3:10-23; 4:7–5:3) are particularly important.

- The particular structure of 2:12-14, employing the word *write/wrote* and the vocative *dear children, fathers, young men* in parallel (2:12-13b NIV; 2:13c-14 KJV). Here the change of the tense of the verb 'write' is noteworthy – present tense in 1:1–2:13, aorist tense in 2:14–5:21. Based on these observations, as well as the above mentioned bracketing and repeated vocabulary, Matthew Jensen suggests a three-part structure for the letter, namely – Introduction (1:1–2:11), Transition (2:12-14) and Body (2:15–5:21).

- The repeated use of the word *know* (thirty-three times in the letter), primarily as an affirmation of the true knowledge of God on the part of the readers, but also as a rebuttal of the so-called knowledge of the secessionists. Closely associated with this are words like *true, truth,* and *real* as opposed to *false, falsehood, lie* and *counterfeit*. It is in this connection that the repeated references in the letter to *obedience / righteousness* (e.g. 2:3-6; 2:28-29; 3:7), *orthodox belief* (e.g. 2:23; 4:15), and *love for the brothers* (3:14; 4:7) are noteworthy. These observations lie at the root of e.g. Stott's proposal that the repetition of these three-fold 'tests of authenticity' (2:3-27; 2:28–4:6; 4:7–5:5) form the heart of the letter's structure.

- The overall use in the letter of repetition, amplification, affirmation, appeal, warning, and present time references (both verb tenses and the use of the word 'now') which Kruse, for example, sees as evidence of a clear praise-and-blame function for the letter (see below). In keeping with this function, one would not expect to find within the letter a structured line of argument but rather a carefully formulated appeal which is best dealt with in terms of its own natural divisions.

Based on a combination of these observations and following, at least in broad terms, the structure suggested by Jensen and Kruse, we will adopt the following division of 1 John (Note only the major divisions are listed here. For a more detailed breakdown see the commentary on 1 John below):

1 John

1:1-4	Fellowship with God
1:5-2:11	Walking in the Light
2:12-14	A Strong Affirmation
2:15-17	The Christian and the World
2:18-27	The Truth and the Lie
2:28-3:10	Children of God
3:11-24	The Gospel of Love
4:1-6	A Call for Discernment
4:7-21	Knowing the Unseen God
5:1-5	The Victorious Life
5:6-12	King on the Cross
5:13-21	That you may know....

What kind of letters are John's Letters?

As noted above, the presence of traditional formulae enables us to identify 2 and 3 John as typical Greco-Roman letters, directed by 'the elder' to a particular congregation ('the chosen lady and her children' – 2 John 1) and a particular individual ('my dear Gaius' – 3 John 1) respectively. Furthermore the brevity and structural and thematic simplicity of the letters make it comparatively easy to discern the primary aim of the author and thus the rhetorical form of the letters. Colin Kruse provides a helpful discussion and concludes that 2 John is a letter designed to exhort, advise, warn and dissuade the readers with respect to their conduct, particularly with reference to their response to those whom the author calls 'deceivers' (2 John 7). 3 John can be classified as a letter written to commend and thus further encourage the recipient, Gaius, in a course of action (support given to those who went out for the Name – 3 John 7), while also gainsaying the conduct of Diotrephes who has chosen the opposite action.

When it comes to 1 John, however, questions regarding form are not so easily resolved. The absence of the traditional beginning or end to 1 John has led some scholars to regard it more as a tract or theological treatise intended for widespread circulation among the churches. According to this view the letter was designed to instruct and correct, though not with particular reference to any particular issue or context. Others point out that the letter does in fact reflect a close relationship between the author and recipients and that its teaching is in direct response to a particular situation created by the destructive and deceptive influence of those whom the author calls 'antichrists' and 'false prophets' (1 John 2:18; 4:1).

In the light of the above, it is probably best to describe 1 John as a circular letter intended for believers in specific congregations with whom the author had a close relationship. The letter serves first to reassure the readers and then to affirm and strengthen them in their adherence to a set of beliefs and an agreed pattern of life, both of which were being challenged by those who had themselves parted company with traditional beliefs and patterns of life and who were now seeking to persuade others to follow them.

2
Why Should we Teach and Preach John's Letters

Theological confusion and uncertainty among believers; moral compromise among those who name the Name of Christ and worse still, who claim to speak for Him; beliefs and behaviour that resemble the prevailing fashions, philosophies and lifestyle of the world rather than those which are consistent with the historic gospel of Jesus Christ; an intolerance of the words such as 'sin' or 'truth'; scepticism about the historicity of Jesus Christ and/or a denial of the centrality and the absolute necessity of His death and resurrection; a lack of discernment and, at times, a naïve gullibility within the church; scarcity of resources for authentic gospel work while false teachers seem to prosper; the lack of sacrificial love among believers; the resurgence of a worldly spirituality which is both mystical and rationalistic – these are just some of the issues that face the church today. The list is, of course, not haphazardly chosen but is in fact a summary of the very issues that John's letters were written to address. And as such it stands as eloquent testimony to why it is more important than ever for John's letters not only to be read but also preached and taught in our churches.

The letters are, as we shall see, both theological and practical. They re-affirm great and central truths about God the Father and the Lord Jesus Christ, truths that are under fire today. But they affirm these truths in a way which is both pastoral and practical, always seeking to work out the application and implication of what Christians have been taught 'from the beginning.' As such they are letters which, carefully taught, will bring both truth and love to bear on those who hear and by God's good grace, will not only feed the sheep but also change the church!

3

Ideas for a Preaching or Teaching Series in John's Letters

Despite their familiarity, the task of preaching a series of sermons or teaching a series of Bible studies in the letters of John is in fact not as straightforward as it might first appear. No sooner has the aspirant preacher turned to the opening paragraph of 1 John, than he is struck by the sheer volume of theological treasures that must be sifted, organised and displayed for all to see. Although John has very helpfully stated his purpose in writing, it is not always easy to see how particular paragraphs contribute to this aim and purpose, and this in conjunction with the rich and varied content of the letter make it quite easy for the preacher either to be distracted and to lose the overall aim from sight, or to flatten out the rich diversity in an attempt to keep the aim of the letter in mind. Add to this John's penchant for repetition, though with subtle variation of emphasis, and the preacher is soon wondering how something that seemed so straightforward in the beginning has become such a tricky task. And yet, as we noted above, these letters are of immense value and importance for the church. So despite the challenges which emerge along the way, committing to teaching or preaching a series in these letters is a very worthwhile and rewarding exercise.

Option 1: A series of consecutive expositions

Given their length, a series of consecutive expositions through the letters does seem to be the optimal approach. A series on 1 John based on the analysis used in this commentary would take about 24 weeks, allowing for the longer sections such as 1:5-2:11 to be dealt with in a series of talks rather than a single sermon. This series can be summarised as follows (see each passage in the commentary for a more detailed breakdown)

Knowing God – Expositions on 1 John

Sermon 1	Fellowship with God	1:1-4	Sermon 13	Confidence before God	3:19-22
Sermon 2	Walking with God	1:5-7	Sermon 14	This is how we know	3:23-24
Sermon 3	The God of Light and the sin of man	1:8-10	Sermon 15	Spiritual discernment	4:1-6
Sermon 4	The Saviour of the world	2:1-2	Sermon 16	Knowing the God who is love	4:7-12
Sermon 5	Knowing the God who is light	2:3-6	Sermon 17	Relying on the God who is love	4:13-16
Sermon 6	The light and the darkness	2:7-11	Sermon 18	Confidence before the God of love	4:16-18
Sermon 7	Blessed Assurance	2:12-14	Sermon 19	Obeying the God who is love	4:19-21

Sermon 8	The Christian and the world	2:15-17	Sermon 20	The Victorious Life	5:1-5
Sermon 9	False or true?	2:18-27	Sermon 21	God's king on the cross	5:6-12
Sermon 10	The way of truth	2:28-3:3	Sermon 22	Encouragement and exhortation	5:13 & 21
Sermon 11	Don't buy the lie	3:4-10	Sermon 23	Confident prayer	5:14-17
Sermon 12	The way of love	3:11-18	Sermon 24	Assured knowledge	5:18-20

As we noted in the introductory comments, in such a longer series of consecutive expositions care must be taken to ensure that each individual exposition is aligned to the author's overall aim and purpose in the letter, namely to build the assurance of true believers and promote their experience of fellowship with God. In this endeavour, it is important however to let each text speak its own message as part of the whole, without flattening out the contours or individual emphases of any one particular text.

Consecutive expositions of 2 and 3 John are more straightforward, though as we shall see below there is also value in doing a short series on these two letters in relationship to each other. A series on each letter, based on the commentary that follows, is summarised below:

The Fellowship of Love and Truth – Expositions on 2 John

Sermon 1	A peculiar people	2 John 1-3
Sermon 2	People of truth and love	2 John 4-6
Sermon 3	True Truth	2 John 7-11
Sermon 4	Face to face	2 John 12-13

Working together for the Truth – Expositions on 3 John

Sermon 1	Gospel friendship	3 John 1
Sermon 2	Gospel Partnership	3 John 2-12
Sermon 3	Make it count	3 John 13-14

Option 2: Thematic studies

Given the theological richness of 1 John and the close relationship that exists in particular between 2 and 3 John, these letters certainly lend themselves to shorter thematic studies.

As far as 1 John is concerned, one obvious series could be based around the twin statements about God that are found in the letter, namely 'God is light' (1 John 1:5) and 'God is love' (1 John 4:16). As we noted in our comments on the structure of 1 John, this is the basic approach that Raymond Brown uses to analyse the message of the letter. For such a series one would focus on the main body of the book, although additional talks could be done on the prologue and the conclusion. The book would be divided into two parts as follows – God is light (1:5–3:10) and God is love (3:11–5:12).

Such a series could look something like the following:

Knowing God – studies about God and the Christian Life from 1 John

Part 1: Knowing the God who is light	Part 2: Knowing the God who is love
A number of talks on key passages taken from 1 John 1:5–3:10	A number of talks based on key passages taken from 1 John 3:11–5:12

As far as a thematic series on 2 and 3 John is concerned, it is worth noting that the key theme in both of the letters is found in the introductory paragraph and centres on the fact that love and truth are inseparable in the life of the individual believer and within the Christian community. Since this is the case, those who walk in the truth should also walk in love. A particular and vitally important application of this is seen in one's attitude toward supporting Christian work.

A series on these two letters together following this theme and application could look something like the following:

Love and Truth – A key lesson from 2 & 3 John

Talk 1: Love and truth are inseparable in 2 John (2 John 1-3)	Talk 2: Love and truth are inseparable in 3 John (3 John 1-4)
Application: Love one another but do not support those who don't preach the truth (2 John 4-11)	Application: Work together for the truth and do support those who preach the truth (3 John 5-14)

Obviously in such thematic series one is being selective and it is important to maintain that discipline in exposition and application. It is also important to show how the thematic approach to these letters does in fact fit in with the overall aim and purpose for which they were written.

Option 3: A series of small group studies on John's letters

In addition to a series of consecutive expositions or thematic studies, John's letters are a great resource for a series of small group studies. The nature of the letter lends itself to such studies with plenty of time to get into the detail of the text and prayerfully apply what John writes.

As with a sermon series, the true believer is enabled to experience true assurance of faith and confidence in his or her relationship with God. Each teaching unit in this book contains a list of questions you could use or adapt for this purpose.

Part 2
Teaching I John

I
FELLOWSHIP WITH GOD (1 JOHN 1:1-4)

Introduction

In the opening paragraph of 1 John we are somewhat abruptly, yet quite wonderfully brought face to face with truth that is both profound and precious. Formal greetings are set aside with the result that the letter, though directed to a specific group, is nevertheless given a universal application. But the lack of formal greeting also has the effect of underlining the urgency and importance of what follows. In words that echo the start of the Fourth Gospel, John directs our attention back to 'the beginning' and to the 'Word of Life' which was 'with the Father', which 'has appeared' and to which John now seeks to bear 'witness'. Familiar Johannine themes abound, yet on closer examination we discover that the opening paragraph of 1 John is not simply a repackaging of the Prologue of the Fourth Gospel.

The focus of the opening paragraph is three-fold:

First, our attention is directed to and fixed upon the Word of Life who appeared in history in the person of

Jesus the Christ. As we shall see, this Jesus centredness is a key feature of the letter, even of those sections which do not deal directly with doctrine.

Second, we are told that the appearance of the Word of Life in history has given rise to the testimony and proclamation of those who were ear- and eye-witnesses, those who like John himself 'heard' and 'saw' and 'touched' the incarnate Word. It is this apostolic witness, in contrast to the confident but spurious claims of the 'liars', which will provide both a firm foundation for fellowship with God and a true basis for Christian assurance.

Third, we are told the reason for the appearance of the Word and thus the first of two great concerns that motivated John to write his letter, namely joyful fellowship with God through Jesus Christ. This fellowship with God, first experienced by John and others who knew Jesus face to face, was not for them alone but indeed for all who would come to know Jesus through their testimony.

Listening to the text

Context and structure

In the original the first three and a half verses of the letter form a single, complex and carefully structured sentence. The subject of the sentence and the primary focus of the writer's interest is 'the Word of Life' (later 'the eternal life' or simply 'the life') which was 'with the Father' but which has now appeared both in the physical world and, more particularly, to John and his associates. The verbal structure of this opening sentence places the emphasis first on the historical appearing of the Life (v. 2a) and then upon the testimony of those to whom the Life first appeared (v. 2b). The twin purpose clauses in verses 3 and

4 seem at first glance to refer to two different objectives. But these clauses are in fact closely connected to each other and to the implied reason for the appearance of the Life. The appearance of the Life, the proclamation of the Life and the purpose of writing are all so that John's readers may in fact share the joyful fellowship with God that John and his associates have found through Jesus who is this Eternal Life.

Although they are as yet unmentioned, it is worth noting that behind John's choice of words and the careful structure of his logic, there stands the spectre of the liars whose own claims to fellowship with God apart from the historical Jesus and the apostolic witness were so unsettling to the church to whom John wrote.

Working through the text

Despite the string of neuter pronouns which describe the object of what John and his associates heard, saw, looked at, touched and proclaimed, it is clear both from the context and from John's choice of words (especially the words looked at and touched) that the object of John's observation and proclamation is Personal rather than abstract or impersonal. John is not describing the dawning of a new philosophical or spiritual insight nor is he announcing the arrival or discovery of a new message to be proclaimed. At the heart of John's personal experience and thus at the heart of his message is the Personal, Divine Word of Life (v. 1, *cf* 1 John 5:20) which has 'appeared' (v. 2).

John begins by telling us that this Word of Life or Life was 'from the beginning' (v. 1) as well as 'with the Father' (v. 2), two descriptions that are surely closely connected to the description of the Personal Word in the Prologue of John's gospel. There the reader was told that the Word 'was in the beginning' and that the Word 'was with God.' (John 1:1). Here, in the introduction to the letter, the reader is told that this same Eternal Life (v. 2) which was always with the Father, has now 'appeared' – that is appeared in history (a reference to the incarnation), and that this Life has 'appeared to us' – that is appeared in particular to John and his associates who were to be the witnesses to the Life (v. 2). It is important to note that the verb 'appeared' is in fact co-ordinate with and not subordinate to the other verbs 'have seen' and 'witness' and 'proclaim' with the result that it is both the appearing of the Life and the witnessing to the Life that form John's main concern in this opening paragraph. As we shall see, this fact of the incarnation of the Life will become one of the major touchstones for orthodoxy and authenticity later in the letter.

It is because the Life appeared to John and his associates in visible and tangible form that they were able not only to hear and see and look at and touch the Life, but also to proclaim the Life to others with accuracy and authority. The verb 'appeared' is used twice in verse 2, at the beginning and the end of the verse, thus bracketing the verbs 'have seen' and 'witness' and 'proclaim'. The implication of this carefully constructed sandwich is that the Life which appeared in the world must of necessity be proclaimed to the world and this by those who had the credentials to do so. This authoritative proclamation stands, of course, in contrast to the words of the false teachers whom we will meet in the rest of the letter.

But John is not simply concerned with the fact of the Word of Life's appearance in history or indeed with the proclamation of the Light for its own sake. John is also deeply concerned with why the Life appeared and thus with why the Life should be proclaimed. John's logic is brilliant and compelling. By means of two purpose clauses (v. 3 and v. 4) John connects the proclamation of what he and his associates 'saw and heard' concerning the Life with his purpose in writing his letter. The letter becomes the confirmation of what was seen and heard and is written for the purpose of shared fellowship and mutual joy. (Our joy (v. 4) is a better reading than 'your joy', but the 'our' is used in an inclusive rather than exclusive sense.)

But this joy of fellowship which John wants to share with the readers is precisely the joy of fellowship with the Father and with His Son Jesus Christ (v. 3). The Life who 'was with the Father' and who has fellowship with the Father appeared in the flesh in the person of Jesus the Christ. The goal of this appearance was that people may once again have fellowship with God, the eternal life for which we were created (v. 2 *cf* John 17:3 and the frequent references to 'knowing God' in the letter). But such fellowship with God is only possible through the One who knows and has fellowship with God the Father and who has now appeared, Jesus the Christ. It was through Jesus and Jesus alone that John and his associates found fellowship with the Father. And it is through Jesus and Jesus alone that others will enter that joyful fellowship as well. The question is thus 'How can those who did not see Jesus face to face have fellowship with Him?' John's answer is simple but breath-taking. Fellowship with Jesus is only possible via fellowship with John and the others who were ear- and eye-witnesses to the Life which appeared in Jesus. For John's first readers and for the subsequent generations, fellowship with God through Jesus Christ takes place only by hearing and believing the apostolic gospel. That is why the Life appeared and why the Life must be proclaimed.

From text to message

As the introduction to John's letter, 1 John 1:1-4 also functions excellently as an introduction to a sermon series on 1 John. Two key truths, each essential for the accomplishment of John's purpose, are introduced. First, a vital link between the Christ of faith and the Jesus of history is established through John's testimony to the appearance of the Divine Word of Life in the person of Jesus Christ. Second, the importance of and the reliability of the apostolic witness is established as a point of reference for Authentic Christian experience. The complexity and theological richness of the passage mean that it is easy to get bogged down in the detail on the one hand or diverted into preaching theological generalities on the other, and so doing, to miss the main point and purpose of the passage which is to introduce us to the reality and means of joyful fellowship with God.

Getting the message clear: the theme

The Word of Life has appeared and has been proclaimed by John and his associates so that we may have authentic fellowship with God the Father through Jesus the Son.

Getting the message clear: the aim

To encourage believers to pursue joyful fellowship with God through faith in Jesus the Christ as we know Him through the apostolic gospel.

A way in

Begin talking about the idea of intimate relationship or close partnership and then tying this to the word 'fellowship'. Raise the possibility of fellowship with God – and the desirability of such fellowship. Ask the questions 'how can such fellowship be real? How can it be real for us?' Point out that it was precisely to bring about this fellowship that John wrote and that by taking what he wrote seriously we too can have the joy of authentic fellowship with God.

A second way in is to approach the passage from the point of view of authority. We live in a world full of claims to spirituality, each of them offering a way to know God. How can these claims be evaluated? Which of them can be trusted? 1 John 1:1-4 presents us with such a claim. The question is, is it a valid claim and, if so, why so? If the claim of 1 John 1:1-4 is valid what does this do to the many claims to spirituality with which we are surrounded?

Ideas for application

- Fellowship with God for each of us is deeply desirable and precious. It is the source of all true joy. It may not be something we want by nature – but it is something we desperately need.
- The coming of Jesus into the world did not only make fellowship with God possible for those who knew Him face to face. It makes fellowship with God possible for us today. All we have to do is to put our trust in Jesus and we can do this because we know Him through what the Bible teaches us about Him. The thing to do is to hear John's words and to act upon them, allowing his words to bring us face to face with Jesus and thus with God.

Suggestions for preaching

Sermon

Fellowship with God (1 John 1:1-4)

1. Introduction
   - The joy of Fellowship
   - The even greater joy of Fellowship with God
2. Fellowship made possible
   - The appearance of the Word of Life, the One who has perfect fellowship with God
   - The proclamation of the Word of Life, the way to fellowship with God for us
3. Entering Fellowship
   - Taking John's words to heart
   - Responding to John's words personally

Suggestions for teaching

Questions to help understand the passage

1. To what or to whom does the phrase 'that which was from the beginning' refer?
2. What titles are used in the passage to describe this One?
3. How does the passage emphasise the reality and the depth of the relationship between the Father and the Word of Life?
4. How does John stress the appearance in history of the Life?

5. What was the purpose of John's testimony about the appearing of the Life and thus of the apostolic preaching? What is surprising about the way this purpose is described in verse 3?
6. According to verse 4, why did John write his letter?
7. How does this purpose in writing connect with John's purpose in testifying to the appearing of the Life?

Questions to help apply the passage

1. Why is fellowship important?
2. What experiences of fellowship give you the most joy?
3. Do you think that it is possible for people to have fellowship with God? If so, then how? If not, then why not?
4. If someone asked you about whether it was possible to know Jesus personally, what would you answer? What reason would you give?
5. Why do you think a relationship with Jesus matters according to this passage?
6. What does this passage teach us about our goal in reading or teaching 1 John?

2
Walking in the Light (1 John 1:5–2:11)

Introduction

The use of the verb 'walk' as a metaphor for a life of fellowship with God, while familiar to readers of the Bible, is nevertheless very striking indeed. The metaphor has its roots in the Old Testament, where we read of Enoch, Noah and Abraham who are said to have 'walked with God' (Gen. 5:24; 6:9) or 'before the LORD' (Gen. 24:40). It is present in God's call upon Israel to '...fear the LORD your God, to walk in all His ways, to love him, to serve the LORD your God with all your heart and with all your soul' (Deut. 10:12 ESV), a call which, to their own loss, they chose to reject because of their stubborn hearts and under the influence of faithless leaders and false prophets.

Given this Old Testament background, it comes as no surprise to find John using this metaphor of a 'walk' to describe the way of life of the authentic follower of Jesus. In 1 John, the metaphor is restricted to 1:5-2:11, where the authentic disciple is described as someone who 'walks in the light' (1:7) and thus 'lives (lit. *remains*) in the light' (2:10), in contrast to those who 'walk in the darkness' (1:6; 2:11) and who 'are still in the darkness' (2:9). The basis of this stark contrast, says John, is the fact that 'God is light and in Him there is no darkness at all' (1:5) with the result that those who have fellowship with God do and will continue to walk in the light, just as Jesus Himself walked (2:6).

As we shall see, the paragraph as a whole is bracketed by the idea of light and darkness (1:5; 2:10,11) and has two subsections, namely, 1:5–2:2 and 2:3-11. The paragraph describes the authentic Christian life as 'life in the light' and is designed to expose the lie of those who claim to be in the light but in fact walk in the darkness and to affirm and encourage those who do indeed walk in the light. It is thus closely aligned with John's overall purpose as expressed in 5:13.

Listening to the text

Context and structure

In 1 John 1:5, the focus shifts from proclamation about the Life who appeared to proclamation of the 'message' that was heard from Him (i.e. the Life). In the original, the word that John uses for 'proclaim' in 1:5 is slightly different to the word used in 1:2-3 and this change in vocabulary, together with the above-mentioned shift of focus, indicates that 1:5 begins a new section of the letter. This fact is further supported by noting that 1:5-6 and 2:10-11 form a literary *inclusio* using the image of light and darkness. The emphasis on authoritative proclamation as well as the reference to fellowship with God (1:6) does, however, underline the continuity of what is being said with what has gone before. The proclamation of the message and the proclamation of the Life are inseparable.

In 1:6-10, we are told that the message proclaimed by John and his associates stands in stark contrast to the 'claims' of the false prophets. At the heart of these claims there is a radical error about the nature of God and thus about the reality and seriousness of sin. The phrase 'if we say' is used three times to set out these spurious claims (1:6,8,10 KJV), the first two being followed by the adversative 'but if we...' (1:7,9) setting out the appropriate counter to the error. In 2:1-2, the focus shifts from the false prophets to the 'little children', and to the provision that has been made for sinners through the propitiation accomplished at the cross by Jesus. Thus teaching about the reality and seriousness of sin as well as teaching about God's provision for sinners dominates this sub-section of the paragraph and ties 1:6–2:2 into a closely argued unit, with 1:5 acting as a link verse to the prologue and as a foundational statement for the argument which follows.

In 2:3-11 the image of light and darkness as a synonym for truth and error is sustained. Along with this John introduces the language of 'knowing' as a description of assurance (2:3,4,5), as well as the criteria of love or hatred as indicators of whether one is in the light or whether one is still in the darkness. Love for the brothers, an example of obedience to His commands (2:3) and in particular 'the new commandment' (2:8), is thus one of the ethical implications of the fact that God is light. As we shall see, however, this theme of love for the brothers as a mark of authenticity is more fully developed in the section of the letter beginning with 3:11 where it is connected to the declaration that God is love (4:8,16).

Working through the text

Fellowship with the God Who is Light (1:5–2:2)

Having established his credentials as a true witness to the Life which has appeared, John now turns his attention to the 'message' which he and his associates 'heard from Him' (i.e. from the Life who appeared) and 'proclaimed' (1:5). At the heart of this message, is the first of two great theological declarations made in the letter: 'God is light; in Him there is no darkness at all' (1:5). The message thus concerns the character of God.

Two things are in view in this declaration about God. First, the declaration that God is light and totally devoid of darkness means that God is true and the one who has made 'the truth' known. This God has done, first in the Word of Life who appeared, then in the message which was heard from him and proclaimed. Those who know God will thus affirm God's truth and walk in the light of that truth because the truth 'is in' them (1:7, *cf* 2:10). By contrast those who deny God's truth, show that the truth in 'not in' them (1:10) and that rather than being in the light, they are in fact still 'in the darkness' (1:6). To claim to know the God who is truth and yet to walk in the darkness is thus to be 'a liar' and not to 'live out the truth' (1:6). Worse still, it is to make him, i.e. the Life who has appeared and who has revealed the truth, 'out to be a liar' (1:10). Whatever such a person may claim, he or she does not in reality have fellowship with the God who is light and truth.

Second, the declaration that God is light and devoid of darkness means that God is perfectly holy and righteous, Himself without sin and thus totally opposed to sin. 'Sin' (the word is used nine times in 1:6–2:2), by its very nature, belongs to the realm of darkness and not to the light. As we shall see below, those who are in the light will therefore acknowledge the truth about sin, stand opposed to sin and pursue purity and righteousness. By contrast, those who are in the darkness deny the truth about sin, claiming 'to be without sin' (1:8) and 'not to have sinned' (1:10). Such claims, far from being evidence that one is truly enlightened, are in fact the very antithesis of the truth and of the light. To make such claims is in fact 'to lie' (1:6), 'to deceive ourselves' (1:8) and to make God out 'to be a liar' (1:10) – strong language indeed, but language which is quite understandable given John's concern for his readers.

What precisely were the secessionists claiming when they claimed to be 'without sin' and 'not to have sinned'? Colin Kruse points out that the phrase 'to have sin' while occurring only here in John's letters, is in fact used four times in John's Gospel (John 9:41; 15:22,24; 19:11), each time with the meaning 'to be guilty of sins'. The claim 'to be without sin' (1:8) was thus not a denial of the reality of sin or a sinful nature, but rather a claim to freedom from the moral guilt which is associated with sin. The claim 'not to have sinned' (1:10) extended this freedom from guilt beyond present conduct to past behaviour. What the secessionists were thus teaching was a gospel which had no place for sin as moral guilt and thus no need for forgiveness or for purification. Deliverance from ignorance rather than from the devastating consequences of sin seems to have been the spiritual salvation that the secessionists were advocating. As we shall see, such a view of sin, of God and of the nature of fellowship with God left no room for a message which proclaimed the necessity of atonement and thus of the incarnation.

What then of John's 'dear children' (2:1) and the authenticity of their fellowship with the God who is light, given the reality of sin and of moral guilt, a reality of which, despite the confident claims of the secessionists they were well aware? John's answer is magnificent. The truth about sin must not be denied nor is sin to be indulged. John's aim in writing is to encourage his readers 'not to sin' (2:1), but, given the reality of sin, also to remind them of God's provision for sinners in the death of Jesus. Jesus Christ, the Righteous One has made propitiation for the sins of the whole world (2:2). Jesus' death and His death alone, provides a way for sinners to be 'forgiven' and 'purified from all unrighteousness' (1:9) (note that 'blood' in 1:7 is a synonym for 'death'). The death of Jesus has thus atoned for sin and removed moral guilt as an obstacle to fellowship with God. But Jesus' death has also removed another obstacle which stands between God and sinners, namely God's righteous wrath against sin. By calling Jesus the 'atoning sacrifice for our sins' (2:2), John thus reminds his readers that the death of Jesus has dealt with every obstacle between them and God. Because of Jesus, sinners can be people of the light and have fellowship with God. Rather than denying sin, true believers acknowledge their sinfulness and confess their actual sins (1:9), trusting in the death of Jesus on their behalf and depending upon Him as their advocate before the Father (2:1). A denial of the reality and the seriousness of sin leads to a false and deadly presumption when it comes to a relationship with God. By contrast, facing the reality of sin and dealing with it through Jesus Christ leads to true and lasting assurance.

What is striking as well is that God's provision, though personal, is not individualistic. Christ's death for sinners means not only that forgiven sinners can know the joy of fellowship with God, but also that they can enjoy 'fellowship with one another' (1:7). When those who claim to be believers walk in the dark and have a lax attitude to sin, the entire community suffers. Those who persist in sin inevitably draw back from service and community. Worse still, their attitude to sin may well cause others to stumble in their relationship with the Lord. According to this passage then, the people of God are a fellowship of forgiven sinners who together seek to walk in the light.

Knowing the God Who is Light (2:3-11)

In 2:3-11, John turns his attention away from the presumptuous and unsettling claims of the secessionists and, for the first time, addresses the question of assurance directly. True believers are now described as those who 'have come to know him' (2:3). Although it is possible to see the word 'him' as a reference to Jesus Christ, the Righteous One in 2:1, it is probably better to take God the Father (1:3), the God who is light (1:5) as the antecedent to 'him' in 2:3. According to John then, authentic believers are those who 'know God the Father' (*cf* 2:14, 4:7). As we shall see in the rest of the letter (e.g. 2:23), and as John has already made abundantly clear in 1:7 and 2:1, such true knowledge of God the Father is never without reference to or possible apart from the Father's Son, Jesus Christ.

But those who truly 'know God' will of necessity also 'keep his commands' (2:3) and 'obey his word' (2:5). John is not, of course, claiming that believers are sinless or that this obedience is perfect. To make such a claim would be to contradict what he has already written about the reality of and remedy for sin. His point is simply that those who truly know God will, in fact, have a new desire and commitment to pursue the very goal and objective that God has for them, namely a way of life which is Christ-like (2:6). It was toward this very goal that 'the love for God' (2:5 NIV footnote), made manifest in sending of Jesus as the atoning sacrifice for the sins of the world (2:2, *cf* 4:9), was directed. And it is thus in this new way of life, exemplified and 'seen in' Jesus (2:6,8), that believers evidence that God's love for them in Christ is 'made complete', that is, has reached its goal. According to John and in contrast to 'lies' of the secessionists (2:4), obedience to God's word is indeed evidence of a true knowledge of God, proof that the word of God dwells in the believer (2:4).

What is true with respect to obedience to God's commands in general will, of course, be true of obedience to the 'new command' in particular. Those who know God will strive to keep his word and obey his commands including the 'new command' to love one another. It would be strange indeed if those who were called to 'live as Jesus did' had no regard for what Jesus himself taught. But, lest he be accused of mere novelty, John makes it clear that the 'new command' which he was writing about and which those who through the gospel had become 'dear friends' (2:7) had heard and accepted 'from the beginning' (2:7), was in fact not new at all. Love for the people of God had always been a characteristic of those who truly know God. What was new was the way in which the command to love had been exemplified and taught by Jesus himself. Jesus' life of sacrificial love was a clear indication of the passing of the darkness and the dawning of the true light (2:8). Those who had truly come to him had thus come out of the darkness, with its deadly stumbling blocks, and into the light. It thus follows that they would 'live in the light' (2:10) and would in turn love their brothers and sisters in Christ (2:9-10), fellow-citizens of the light. Love for one's brothers and sisters in Christ is thus further evidence that one does indeed belong to the light and know the God who is light. Conversely, those who hate the brothers and sisters in Christ show that they are still in the darkness (2:9, 11). Far from being spiritually enlightened as they claimed to be, they were in fact spiritually blind (2:11), strangers to the God who is light.

From text to message

Although 1 John 1:5–2:11 comprises a literary and thematic unit, the length and the theological richness of the passage mean that it is unlikely that the passage can be dealt with in a single talk. The overarching theme of light and darkness and the key theological truth that God is light do, however, make the passage ideal for a short series, keeping in mind, of course, that the main theme and the aim of the passage as a whole should be kept in mind during each individual exposition. Given the many and varied claims that are made for a genuine relationship with God, frequently, however, without any reference to the problem of sin, the centrality of the death of Jesus or the need for what, in an earlier generation, was called a 'credible profession of faith', a series on 1 John 1:5–2:11 will no doubt prove to be both an encouragement to true believers and a necessary corrective to those whose claims to know God are nothing more than a false and, in the end, a spiritually fatal presumption.

Getting the message clear: the theme

Because God is light, those who walk in the light, and they alone, are the true 'knowers of God'. To walk in the light means:-

- To live in the light of the truth of God, including the unpalatable truth about sin.
- To live in obedience to God's commands.
- To live with love toward fellow believers.

Getting the message clear: the aim

To counter false claims to a relationship with God and to encourage and assure true believers in their commitment to a gospel-shaped relationship with God.

A way in

The idea of the Christian life as a 'walk' is a very rich and compelling idea, particularly for post-moderns. Use this idea to introduce the short series but remind the hearers that when John uses this image to describe the Christian life what is in view, of course, is not an aimless meander in the company of a friend, but a journey: a journey along a set path and with a definite destination; a journey which requires perseverance and proven character; a lifelong journey undertaken not in isolation but in the company of others, supremely in the company of One who leads and who not only knows the way but who is the Way. True believers are those who walk in the light, just as Jesus walked in the light. In practice this means that they walk in truth, in righteousness and in love. Each individual talk in the series can then explore each of these aspects of the 'walk'.

A second way in for the introductory talk in the series is via John's use of light and darkness. The idea of being an enlightened person has great appeal today. But what does it mean to be 'enlightened'? Who gets to determine what is light and what is darkness? According to John, the only one who can define light and darkness is God himself, because he alone is light. And God's definition of enlightenment is very different from ours for it goes beyond mere knowledge to life and it affirms rather than denies the reality of right and wrong. The truly enlightened person is thus the person who knows the God who is light and who walks in the light that God gives.

Having introduced the series as a whole, one will, of course, need to plan each talk within the series. For talk 1, based upon 1:5-10, one way in is to point out that if we want to walk in the light, we first need to come into the light. This we do by facing the truth about sin, by coming to see sin in general and our own sin in particular not as the world sees sin, but as God sees it. The world and the worldly church deny the reality and the deadly consequences of sin and they thus see the teaching about the death of Jesus as irrelevant at best, abhorrent at worst. By contrast, those who come into God's light and walk in God's light deal with sin in the way that God has provided, namely, through the atoning death of Jesus.

A way in for talk 2, based upon 2:1-2 could be to note the difficulty that the reality of sin causes believers. Sin troubles the conscience and rightly so, but it also shakes our assurance. How can and should believers deal with sin? Rather than deny sin we should acknowledge sin and fight sin, yet always from the knowledge that it is Jesus who, on the basis of his atoning death, secures our relationship with God.

A way in for talk 3, based on 2:3-11 could be to define the true Christian as someone who knows God. However, many today claim that they know God, a fact which means that such claims must be tested and validated. How can the believer truly know that he or she knows God? In 2:3-11, John provides us with a sound basis for knowing that we truly know God. Those who know will love God's word and do it and they will love God's people. This is the example that Jesus set and thus it is the way of life that true believers will follow. Of course, one may prefer to deal with this passage in two parts, namely 2:3-6 and 2:7-11.

Ideas for application

- Although the world and the worldly church deny the reality and seriousness of sin, John makes it absolutely clear that sin is real and deadly. And yet it is also clear from John's teaching that sin need not keep people away from God. This section of 1 John thus gives us great opportunities to talk about sin and how to deal with it.
- Closely related to the above is, of course, John's teaching about the death of Jesus in 1:5–2:2. The passage thus provides an ideal opportunity to explain the atonement, both in relation to sin and in relation to the wrath of God, and to counter the teaching of those who deny the necessity and centrality of the atonement.
- The question of assurance remains central to the passage as a whole. In particular, it gives an opportunity to address the relationship between sin, obedience and assurance.

Suggestions for preaching

Series Title: Walking in the Light (1 John 1:5–2:11)

Sermon 1

Walking with God (1:5-7)

1. The truth about God

    - God is light
    - There is no darkness in God

2. The Christian walk

    - A call to walk in the light
    - A call to walk in fellowship with God
    - A call to walk in fellowship with one another

Sermon 2
The God of Light and the sin of man (1:5-10)

1. The truth about God

    - God is light
    - There is no darkness in God

2. The truth about sin

    - Sin separates
    - Sin must be faced
    - Sin can be forgiven

3. The truth about people

    - All have sinned
    - Deceived and deceivers
    - Forgiven sinners

Sermon 3
The Saviour of the World (2:1-2)

1. A World in need of salvation

    - A world ensnared by sin
    - A world lost in the dark

2. The Saviour of the World
   - Jesus Christ the Righteous One
   - An Atonement for sins
   - An Advocate with the Father

Sermon 4
Knowing the God who is light (2:3-6)

1. The God who can be known
   - The love of God at work
   - The word of God at work
2. The people who know their God
   - Claims – true and false
   - Keeping His word
   - Following His Son

Sermon 5
The Light and the Darkness (2:7-11)

1. The dawning of the light
   - Truth seen in Him
   - Truth at work in us
   - Things old and new
2. Life in the Light
   - The mark of darkness
   - The people of the light

Suggestions for teaching

Questions to help understand the passage

1. What does this passage teach about God?
2. What does the statement 'God is light' mean with respect to
   - Truth?
   - Righteousness?
3. Why did John state the counterpoint 'in Him is no darkness at all'?
4. What did the secessionists claim?
5. How did John counter their claims on each occasion?
6. What does 1:5–2:11 teach us about the secessionists, their beliefs and actions?
7. What does 1:5–2:11 teach us about the true Christian life?
8. What do we learn from 1:5–2:2 about the Person and Work of Jesus?
9. In what way does John use the word 'know' in this passage?
10. What is the sign that God's love has been made complete (i.e. reached its goal) in the life of a believer?
11. In what way is the command to love one another
    - Old?
    - New?

12. What does John mean when he uses the word 'stumble'?

13. In what way does John use the images of light / darkness in this passage?

Questions to help apply the passage

1. How should believers respond to the reality of sin?

2. How does sin affect assurance?

3. How does sin affect our relationship with our fellow-believers?

4. How do the death and intercession of Jesus enable us to be in fellowship with God?

5. How does a life of obedience and of love for fellow-believers assure Christians of their relationship with God?

6. How would you use this passage in a conversation with

   - A nominal Christian?
   - A Christian struggling with some besetting sin?
   - A Christian who doubts their relationship with God?

3
A Strong Affirmation (1 John 2:12-14)

Introduction

Although 1 John 2:12-14 is sometimes referred to as a 'digression', a careful look at the passage and its vocabulary shows that it is in fact absolutely core to John's purpose in writing and of the utmost importance for his appeal to his readers. Over and against the unsettling claims of the secessionists, John provides his readers with his own assessment of their spiritual condition. Unlike the claims of the secessionists, this assessment is in no way presumptuous, for it is based upon the fact that those whom John addresses do in fact 'believe in the name of the Son of God' (5:13, *cf* 2:12). In a carefully crafted, three-fold affirmation he assures them that having been forgiven in Jesus' name, they now know 'Him who is from the beginning' (i.e. Jesus – 2:13a,14b) and, as a result, they truly know and have fellowship with the Father (2:14a). In addition to this, indeed by virtue of this forgiveness and fellowship, they also have victory over the evil one, his onslaughts and accusations, in whatever form these may occur (2:13b,14c). Thus assured and empowered by the indwelling word of God, they are fully equipped to overcome the world and to stand firm to the very end.

Listening to the text

Context and structure

Even a cursory glance at 1 John 2:12-14 makes it clear that the passage has been very carefully structured by the author. The passage consists of two parallel and symmetrical triads (vv. 12-13 and v. 14) in which each sentence begins with a reference to the author's act of writing, followed by a particular form of address and a prepositional clause indicating not purpose or content but the reason for writing. The change of the tense of the verb 'to write' from simple present to the so-called 'epistolary aorist' in v. 14 was in all likelihood both for stylistic and rhetorical reasons, probably to underline that what had been written still stands as present truth for the readers.

Although John had addressed his readers directly on two previous occasions, namely 2:1 ('dear children') and 2:7 ('dear friends'), the repeated use of the direct form of address – *dear children, fathers, young men* – coupled with the repeated use of the verb *I am writing*...has the effect of arresting the reader's attention and directing it in particular to the explanatory clauses which follow each statement. In each case these explanatory clauses are descriptive not prescriptive, and thus set out John's own assessment of his readers. This fact serves to align the passage closely with John's overall aim in writing.

Functionally, the passage acts as a bridge between the first part of the letter (1:5–2:11) with its declaration of the true message spelt out in terms of the contrast between *light* and *darkness*; *the truth* and *the lie*, and the second part of the letter (1 John 2:15–5:21) which warns against the *world* in all its manifestations, and in particular against the teaching of the false prophets and antichrists who, as we shall see, speak not from the viewpoint of the Father, but from the viewpoint of the world (*cf* 4:5). Linguistically, the passage echoes key words from 1:5–2:11, for example, 'sin', 'forgiveness', 'know', 'beginning', and the 'indwelling word', words which, as we shall see, recur at different points in 2:15–5:21. But the passage also introduces key words that will be used in 2:15–5:21, for example, 'name', 'evil one', and 'overcome'.

Working through the text

As we have seen, John's exposition of the truth about God in 1:5–2:11 was intended not merely to counter the false claims of the secessionists, but, in the process, also to provide the basis for true assurance among believers. Such assurance, while deeply personal, was not subjective and had to be based upon objective criteria, most notably the death of Jesus as the atoning sacrifice for the sins of the whole world (2:2). In 2:12-14, John moves from more general exposition to direct address and affirmation of his readers. But in doing so he is careful to base his affirmation of them upon objective grounds and in particular upon the accomplishment of Christ – the one who is 'from the beginning' (2:13; 14b).

It is clear from the letter as a whole that the form of address 'dear children' (2:12a, 14a) does not simply apply to a specific group among the readers, but to all true believers (*cf* 2:1,18, 28; 3:7,18; 4:4; 5:21). Such a designation clearly underlines the intimacy of John's own relationship with his readers, but it also reflects their status as children of God the Father (e.g. 3:1-2; 5:2) and thus as brothers and sisters to one another (e.g. 2:10, 3:10). Given this fact, it is then highly unlikely that the terms 'fathers' (13a, 14b) or 'young men' (13b, 14c) refer to different levels of spirituality of the kind that the super-spiritual secessionists were claiming or promoting among the readers. The terms, which are exclusive to 2:12-14, should rather be understood to designate two specific groups, the older and younger members of the church, which together made up the congregation as a whole. In each case the description which follows is appropriate to the title – long standing relationship with the Lord for those who are older, strength and vigour for those who are younger – but as we shall see below, there is no essential distinction drawn as regards the quality of each group's relationship with Christ. Indeed, each of the descriptions highlights one aspect of what is true for every true believer, namely forgiveness leading to a true relationship with the Lord and spiritual strength to withstand the onslaught of the world, the flesh and the devil. In the final analysis then, the repetition of the three forms of address – dear children, fathers, young men – while adding texture to the description has the effect of applying what is said of each group to all of John's readers.

As we noted above, the focus of the passage is in particular upon the six prepositional clauses which state why John has written and in the process affirm six key things that are true of John's readers. When placed in parallel to each other it is clear that the central affirmation of each triad is identical – *lit* 'I write to you fathers because you have known him who is from the beginning'. This is a reference not to the Father, but rather to Jesus, the eternal

Son who appeared (1:1-4). The use of the perfect tense, here and in each of the clauses refers to an event which, though in the past, has present consequences. Conversion to Christ brings every believer into a personal relationship with Christ, a relationship which continues throughout life and on into eternity.

But conversion to Christ and the relationship with Christ that follows is itself based upon the full forgiveness that comes to sinners 'on account of his (i.e. Jesus') name' (2:12). Here as elsewhere in the New Testament, the 'name' is shorthand for the person and the work of the one whose name it is. Later in the letter, John identifies Christians as those who 'believe in the name' of the Son of God, Jesus Christ (3:23; 5:13). Here, in particular, he has in mind the death of Jesus which brings forgiveness to all who believe in His name (1:7–2:2). In the parallel statement made to the 'dear children' in verse 14a, John affirms that they 'have known the Father'. Again the emphasis is upon a relationship which having begun at a certain moment, continues into the future. If we compare the two parallel statements addressed to the 'dear children' we conclude that the act of forgiveness which came to them in the name of Jesus and led to relationship with Jesus (vv. 13a; 14b), is then also the foundation of the relationship which they have with the Father. As we shall see later in the letter, this link between knowing Jesus the Son and knowing the Father is of the utmost importance to John.

The final affirmation in each triad is addressed to the 'young men'. In both verses 13b and 14c, they are said to have 'overcome the evil one'. The perfect tense of the verb links this victory over the evil one to a past event, in context, the forgiveness of sins in Jesus' name. But it also implies that the victory is ongoing, and in verse 14c we have the additional description 'you are strong and the word of God lives in you'. This is the only use of the adjective 'strong' in the letter and thus the meaning of the word is best understood from the immediate context. If we understand the 'and' epexegetically, then it is the indwelling word, itself the result of forgiveness and relationship with the Father through the Son, that gives the 'young men' and indeed all the readers, the strength and the victory over the evil one.

In summary then, the passage as a whole is a clear affirmation of every one of the believers. The bold claims of the secessionists may have unsettled John's readers, but such presumptuous and unfounded claims should not be allowed to undermine the assurance that is the birthright of everyone who has trusted in Jesus' name, who has been forgiven, who knows the Son and the Father and who has thus overcome the evil one. In the final analysis, John's assessment, founded on the great truths of the gospel, must hold sway. And, as we shall see, it is this confident and well-founded assessment that will provide the foundation for the life of victory over the world to which all true believers are called.

From text to message

As we have already noted in the Introduction, those passages in which John refers directly to his act of writing are of key importance, providing insight to John's primary concerns as well as his key beliefs. The declaration 'you have known him who was from the beginning' puts particular emphasis on Christ, reminding the reader that He is central to authentic relationship with God. It is in his name that sins are forgiven and a relationship with the Father is not only possible, but actual. And it is only through knowing Him and the Father that the evil one is overcome and that a life of victory can follow. In preaching this passage then, it is absolutely imperative that Christ be kept central to the message so that the assurance that flows from such affirmation as we find in 2:12-14, is indeed based on Christ's accomplishment alone.

Getting the message clear: the theme

Those who have been forgiven in Jesus' Name and on the basis of his atoning death are the ones who truly know the Son and thus the Father. At the moment of our conversion to Christ we have victory over the evil one and are given the resources through the indwelling word of God to live in victory.

Getting the message clear: the aim

To assure believers in Jesus that they have indeed been forgiven in Jesus' name and that they do thus have an authentic relationship both with Jesus and the Father, irrespective of the doubts that they may experience from time to time. Such doubts are in fact the work of the evil one but in Christ he has been overcome and can be resisted.

A way in

Given that this is the first passage within 1 John which directly addresses the issue of assurance, this topic should provide the way in to the exposition of the text. One can begin by talking about the importance of assurance, particularly its importance for confidence in prayer and witness and as a safeguard for the believer against the confident but erroneous talk of the false teacher. By contrast, lack of assurance can easily undermine prayer, stifle evangelistic zeal and make those who feel these doubts more susceptible to 'new' teachings which promise much but which in the end deliver nothing of lasting value. Experience also teaches us that lack of assurance is a problem with which all believers struggle from time to time and it is worth mentioning this by way of introduction. In this regard it is striking that John addresses this issue in relation to the whole community of believers, not just a particular group such as the young or the young in the faith.

Ideas for application

- The concept of assurance can easily be confused with an inappropriate presumption. And so it would be, if it were based on our performance. It is, however, clear from this passage that all true assurance flows out of Christ's work on the cross. Founded upon Christ, true assurance is not only possible but available to every believer.

- The passage once again underlines the vital connection between a relationship with Christ and a relationship with the Father. John makes it clear that it is only by knowing Christ (He who was from the beginning), that believers know the Father. Without the Son, a relationship with the Father is impossible (see also 2:22-23; 4:15; 5:11-12). Given our pluralistic society, it is of the utmost importance that this truth be taught as one of the cornerstones of authentic Christianity.

- Much is made in some Christian circles about 'spiritual warfare' and victory over the evil one.

This passage addresses the issue in a very striking way, linking our victory over evil and the evil one, first with Christ's accomplishment on the cross, particularly the liberating and transforming power of forgiveness, and secondly with the power of God's Word in the heart of the believer.

Suggestions for preaching

The following outline covers the passage as a whole. It is, however, quite possible to preach a short series on this passage highlighting (1) Assurance, its true nature and basis; (2) The saving and liberating power of forgiveness; (3) The vital link between knowing Christ and knowing the Father; (4) The victorious Christian Life as rooted in forgiveness, relationship with Christ and the power of the indwelling Word of God.

Sermon

Blessed Assurance (1 John 2:12-14)

1. Introduction
   - Assurance or Presumption?
   - Assurance for all
2. A True Foundation for Assurance
   - Sins forgiven in His Name
   - Knowing Christ – Knowing God
3. Fear no evil
   - Victory at the Cross
   - The Liberating power of Forgiveness
   - The Power of the indwelling Word

Suggestions for teaching

Questions to help understand the passage

1. To whom is John referring in the description 'dear children'? (2:12,14; see also 2:1,28; 3:7,18; 4:4; 5:21)
2. If the title 'dear children' is John's description for the whole congregation, then to whom do the titles 'fathers' and 'young men' refer?
3. Given the symmetry of the passage, how do John's explanatory statements relate to each other? For example – how are the two statements made about the dear children, i.e. 'your sins have been forgiven on account of his (Jesus') name' and 'you have known the Father' connected?
4. In what way is 'knowing the One who is from the beginning' connected to 'knowing the Father'?
5. How was /is victory over the evil one secured?

Questions to help apply the passage

1. Is assurance important? Why?
2. Is assurance possible? How?
3. What does this passage teach us about the difference between true assurance and arrogant presumption?
4. How does this passage answer those who claim that it is possible to know God without Christ?
5. What resources has God given to us in our fight against the evil one?

6. In the light of this passage, what is there:

    - To thank God for?
    - To act upon?
    - To share with others?

4
The Christian and the World (1 John 2:15-17)

Introduction

In 1 John 2:15-17, we move from declaration (1:1-2:11) and affirmation (2:12-14) to exhortation and warning. The passage marks the beginning of the second and main part of the letter (see *Context and Structure* below) and raises a primary concern of John's, namely that of the relationship between true believers and the fallen world within which they live. In its own right, the passage is one of the 'purple' passages within the letter. In language which echoes the teaching of Jesus in John 14-17, the passage highlights two clear and strongly opposed dualities – first, love for the Father as opposed to love for the world (2:15); second, the transitory nature of the world and its desires as opposed to the eternal life that is the possession and certain hope of all who do the Father's will (2:17). The passage also provides us with a striking definition of what 'love for the world' entails (2:16).

Listening to the text

Context and structure

Although a number of commentaries link 1 John 2:15-17 with the preceding paragraph and view it either as part of a digression or as transitional material, it is preferable to see 1 John 2:15-17 as the introduction to the second and main part of the letter. As Matthew Jensen points out, the word 'world' which occurs in v. 15, is in fact a key word in 1 John 2:15-5:21. Of the twenty three occurrences of the word in 1 John, only one is in the section from chapter 1:1 to chapter 2:14. And even in this one case (1 John 2:2), the word is not used in the pejorative sense that it has in the second half of the letter. In 1 John 2:2 as in 4:14, the world is seen as the object of the love of the Father who 'sent His one and only Son into the world' (4:9) to be the atoning sacrifice for the sins of the world (2:2) and thus to be the world's one and only saviour (4:14). As we shall see, in all other occurrences the word 'world' is used with the same negative connotations that it has in 2:15.

This negative view of the world also enables us to see the close connection between 2:15-17 and 2:18-27. In the latter passage John issues an urgent warning against the teaching of those who, if given a sympathetic hearing, will lead the believers astray (2:26). These false prophets, as John later calls them (4:1), are in fact 'from the world and therefore speak from the viewpoint of the world' with the result that 'the world listens to them' (4:5). By contrast those who are from God should not love the world and thus not listen to the persuasive but worldly words of these false teachers. The connection between 2:15-17 and 2:18-27 is, of course, also evident from the time element that is found in 2:17

and 2:18. Since the world and everything in it is passing away (2:17) the believers find themselves living in 'the last hour' (2:18).

The fact that 1 John 2:15-17 forms the introduction to the second part of the letter, does not, however, mean that it has no connection with the paragraph that immediately precedes it. In 2:12-14, John twice described authentic believers as those who 'have overcome the evil one'. Later in the letter, John declares that 'the whole world is under the control of the evil one' (5:19). Thus it comes as no surprise that John, who as we have already seen was very conscious of the reality of remaining sin in the hearts of true believers, should warn those who in Christ have overcome the evil one, to stand firm against the allure of the world which is his domain and a real source of temptation.

Structurally, the passage consists of an opening exhortation (v. 15a), followed by a three-fold declaration (vv. 15b-17). The exhortation and the final declaration (v. 17) are closely connected and are arranged symmetrically around the central declaration (v. 16) which is explanatory of each.

Working through the text

That the language of 'world' dominates this short passage can be clearly seen from the fact that it is used four times in the space of three verses. As noted above, the word only occurs once in the preceding section, so this focus on the 'world' is clearly a new and important emphasis within the letter. Whereas in the earlier occurrence, the world was seen to be the beneficiary of Christ's saving work and thus by implication, the object of the Father's love (*cf* 4:9-10), the word is used in 1 John 2:15-17 solely with negative connotations. As we have already noted, these negative connotations are spelt out by John throughout the second part of the letter. In 2:15-17, however, he raises two fundamental and closely related points about why the true believer should love neither the world nor the things of the world.

First, says John, such love of the world and the things that are in the world, is the very antithesis of 'love of the Father' (v. 15b). As with all genitive constructions, the reader must decide on the basis of the context, what the phrase 'of the Father' refers to. Is it the love that the Father has, the love that the Father gives, or love for the Father? In the present context, it seems best to opt for the latter as most translations in fact do. Of course, such 'love for the Father' is far more than an attitude or something to which one can pay mere lip service. Throughout 1 John, love always finds expression in action (see e.g. 3:16-18) and 1 John 2:15-17 is no exception. Those who love the Father will therefore, of necessity, do the Father's will (2:17 *cf* 2:5; 5:2-3).

But those who love the Father and desire to do His will also stand opposed to everything that is 'not from the Father' (2:16). This must then be true when it comes to the things that 'are in the world'. In 2:15 John simply mentions these things, but in the following verse they are defined in striking terms. First, there is 'the lust of the flesh'. Although this phrase does include particular lusts, it should not be reduced to these. Rather it is a reference to being ruled and governed by self rather than God, one's own desires rather than the will of God. As we saw in 2:14, one of the characteristics of those who know the Father is that the word of God dwells in them. In the light of this, we can thus say that being governed by the 'lust of the flesh' is the antithesis of being ruled by the indwelling word of

God. Secondly, the 'things that are in the world' refers to the 'lust of the eyes'. Here John has in mind a life governed by materialism and greed, a life that is ruled by what is seen and what can be touched. The Father is, of course, the giver of all good gifts and this includes material gifts. But a life ruled by material things is the very antithesis of a life of love for the Father. Indeed, it is the very essence of idolatry (*cf* 5:21). Thirdly, and finally, 'the things that are in the world', includes what John describes as 'the pride of life'. By this he is referring to a boastful, self-centred pride which lacks humility before God and which lifts itself up above others. Such boastfulness, confident in its denials and presumptuous in its claims, was doubtless a characteristic of the secessionists whom John will tackle head on in the next section.

The second reason John gives as to why believers should not love the world or the things of the world, is found in 2:17 – 'the world and its desires will pass away but whoever does the will of God lives for ever'. At face value, the verse is simply a contrast between the eternal life which all who know and love the Father enjoy, and the temporary nature of the world and its desires. But behind these words there is a very important truth and a very strong warning. The appearance of Christ did indeed deal with sin, overcome the evil one and bring eternal life to all who trust in His name. But it also inevitably ushered in the reality of God's judgement on all that is evil and all that stands in opposition to God. As John puts it in 3:8: 'the reason the Son of God appeared was to destroy the devil's work'. Since the world (in the pejorative sense) and everything that belongs to it, is under the control of the evil one (5:19), it must therefore also be destroyed in the righteous judgement of God. Given that this is true, it is thus unthinkable that anyone who knows and loves the Father would also love that to which the Father is implacably opposed. As for Jesus, so for John; the true believer cannot love both God and the world.

From text to message

1 John 2:15-17 is indeed a 'purple' passage and as such it can easily be taught without reference to the argument of the letter. As we mentioned above, the issue of the Christian and the world is one of the primary concerns of the second part of the letter as a whole, not just of 1 John 2:15-17. This means that in expounding the passage we must, on the one hand, be governed by what the passage itself says about the world and the challenge that the world poses, taking care not to import what John says elsewhere about the world. On the other hand, we must remember that the passage is part of a larger context and so take care to relate it to what immediately precedes and to what follows. In particular, three key points about the believer and the world should be emphasised: First, the world with its desires, its values and its point of view is diametrically opposed to God. Second, the world with its desires, values and point of view is totally opposed by God and is therefore passing away. Third, given the nature and the future of the world, those who have come to love God and desire to do His will must of necessity resist the pull of the world and stand firm for God. Having overcome the evil one because of what Christ has done and in the strength of His indwelling word, they are now to overcome the pull of the world. As part of this, as the next passage will show, they will have to withstand the false teaching

of those who speak from the world and thus against God and His Christ.

Getting the message clear: the theme

The godless world, with its values, viewpoints and desires stands in stark opposition to God and His good and perfect will. It therefore stands under the judgement of God and will pass away. The true believer, who has come to love God, and who thus desires to obey God, must no longer give allegiance to the world or be ruled by the world.

Getting the message clear: the aim

To remind believers of the incompatibility of love for God and love for the godless world and to warn them against being drawn back into love for the world.

A way in

One way in is to remind hearers of the powerful hold that the world has upon us by nature. We are so easily governed by what we see and ruled by what we want. We so easily define ourselves in worldly terms. Along with the evil one, the 'world' and the 'flesh' are indeed the enemies of the soul. As believers in Christ we do have a new affection, a new allegiance and an eternal hope. But we also still live 'in the world' and are vulnerable to its pull upon our hearts. The world will attempt to shape our beliefs (even our religious beliefs) and it will find subtle ways to shape our lives. For this reason we need to be reminded that the world is indeed at war with God and God is at war with the world but that in the end God wins and the world will be judged. With this in mind, we need to be urged to set our hearts and minds not on what the world teaches and offers but on what is godly and will last for eternity.

Another way in is to contrast the good world which God in His love created and the good gifts which God in his love gives to us with the godless world and its enslaving demands. In God's good design, we were meant to enjoy his gifts with freedom. In the fallen world, God's good gifts become perverted by our sinfulness and freedom gives way to bondage. Far from being free, we are ruled by our desires, by material things and by what others think about us. But in this broken world, God in His love has intervened to win back our hearts and to give us true freedom and hope. Being a Christian means being able to say NO to the world and YES to God.

Ideas for application

- Victory over the evil one in and through Christ must necessarily lead to a commitment to resist the desires, values and points of view of the godless world.
- The reality of our relationship with God can be measured by taking honest stock of our own hearts. What rules our minds and hearts and shapes our decisions? Are we ruled by what we want, what we see, or the image of self that we wish to project? Or are we ruled by the word of God and characterised by grateful contentment?
- As human beings we are so often governed by the material and the immediate. However as Christians we are called to be governed by the will and Word of God and to live every day in the light of eternity.
- By nature we love the world, but by grace we are called to love God.

Suggestions for preaching

Sermon

The Christian and the World (1 John 2:15-17)

1. Introduction
    - The challenge we face – fallen people in a fallen world
    - The calling we have – God's people with an eternal hope
2. The world and its desires
    - The lust of the flesh – ruled by what I want
    - The lust of the eyes – ruled by what I see
    - The pride of life – defined and affirmed by the world
3. The problem with the world
    - A world at war with God
    - A world that is passing away
4. The privilege of every believer
    - A new and powerful affection
    - A new and liberating obedience
    - A new and transforming hope
5. The call to every believer
    - Do not love the world or anything in the world
    - Live for eternity

Suggestions for teaching

Questions to help understand the passage

1. How does John's use of the word 'world' in 2:15-17 differ from the use of the word in 2:2?
2. Is John's view of the world positive or negative in this passage?
3. What three things constitute 'everything in the world'?
4. How would you define each of these aspects of the 'world'?
5. What two dualities or contrasts does John describe in this passage?
6. What are the two fundamental problems with the world according to this passage?
7. Why must believers not love the world?

Questions to help apply the passage

1. In what way does the world exercise its hold over us?
2. Why is the world so hard to resist?
3. Is it possible for Christians to love God and love the world?
4. What is the most powerful antidote to 'love of the world'?
5. What two things must we bear in mind when we feel the pull of the world?
6. What encouragement does this passage give us in our fight against the pull of the world?

5
The Truth and the Lie (1 John 2:18-27)

Introduction

Although the secessionists have been in his mind from the very beginning of the letter, it is only in 1 John 2:18-27 that John addresses the problem of the secessionists directly for the first time. As we may expect, John directs his attention to both doctrine and conduct in his attempt to warn his readers against the influence of those who are 'trying to lead you astray' (v. 26). Doctrinally, these people are 'liars' and 'antichrists' (v. 22), having turned their backs on the apostolic truth that was taught and heard 'from the beginning' (v. 24). In practice, they are secessionists, those who have broken fellowship with the true gospel community, choosing rather to go their own way (v. 19) and to lead others after them (v. 26).

But, as important as John's warning against the influence of the secessionists is, it is also clear that John's aim in this paragraph, as elsewhere in the letter, is to assure his readers of the reality of their own relationship with both the Father and the Son and to encourage them to stand firm in that relationship (v. 27). As believers in Jesus the Christ, they live in a fallen and hostile world and in 'the last hour' (v. 18). But they also live in true fellowship with the Lord and His people, a reality to which the 'anointing', the Holy Spirit Himself, testifies (vv. 20, 27). Because of this true fellowship with the Father and the Son, even in the midst of a hostile world, they can stand firm against the misleading words of those who offer false hope and stand assured in the promise of eternal life (vv. 24, 25).

Listening to the text

Context and structure

Although the direct form of address 'Dear children' (v. 18) clearly marks the beginning of a new section, the declaration 'this is the last hour' (v. 18), links back to the statement in 2:17 that 'the world and its desires pass away'. Likewise, the declaration that the one who 'does the will of God lives forever' (2:17), ties in very closely with the exhortation to 'remain in Him' (vv. 24, 27) and with the promise of 'eternal life' (v. 25). Furthermore, the warning against the 'love of the world' in 2:15 leads naturally to a paragraph which warns against the deceptive influence of those who, as we shall see later, speak 'from the viewpoint of the world' (4:5). Finally, we note that although the references in 2:28 to 'continuing' in Christ and to the 'coming' of Christ do connect closely with the reference to the 'last hour' and the importance of 'remaining' in Christ, the direct form of address 'dear children' in 2:28 does serve to delineate 2:28–3:10 as a new and distinct paragraph.

As far as the structure of the paragraph is concerned, opinions vary. The references in v. 20 and v. 27 to the 'anointing' and the twin references to John's act of writing

(vv. 21, 26) suggest that vv. 20-27 should be treated as a unit in which John seeks to assure his readers of the authenticity of their beliefs. According to this view, vv. 18-19 serves as an introductory statement identifying the secessionists with the antichrist. However, the reference to the 'antichrist' in v. 22 and the play on words between 'went out' and 'going' (v. 19), on one hand, and 'remain' (vv. 24, 27) on the other, suggests that the paragraph as a whole is closely connected and should be treated as a single unit.

Working through the text

The words 'Dear children' with which the paragraph begins would have had a two-fold effect on John's original readers. First, as a direct form of address, they draw the attention of the readers to what follows, in this case a statement identifying the secessionists with the antichrist of the 'last hour'. Second, the words 'dear children' serve to confirm the status of the readers both in their relationship with John himself and in their relationship with the Father. As members of the gospel community and those who 'know the truth' (vv. 20, 21), truth that was taught 'from the beginning' (v. 24), they are John's spiritual children and part of the gospel community. In this they stand in stark contrast to those who 'went out' (v. 19) and so doing cut themselves off from the community. But as those who have 'an anointing from the Holy One' and who 'know the truth' (v. 20), they are also 'dear children' in the sense that they are God's children (*cf* 3:1,2,10). Thus in this form of address John is also reassuring his readers of their status with God and in the true gospel community in contrast to the status of those who have left and who are trying to draw others away as well (v. 26).

The words 'the last hour' (v. 18) are unique to John and in all likelihood an equivalent to the words 'the last days' found elsewhere in the New Testament, a reference to an indeterminate period of time, ushered in by the coming of the Christ and consummated at his return. The words have a three-fold function in the paragraph. First, they underline the truth that the 'world and its desires' are indeed 'passing away' (2:17), thus reinforcing John's appeal to his readers to not 'love the world'. Second, they identify the appearance of the secessionists (v. 19) with the coming of the expected 'antichrist' (v. 18) so that the readers will not be lead astray by them. Third, they underline the fact that with the appearance of Jesus the last hour has indeed dawned, thus demonstrating that Jesus is the Christ, the very truth that the secessionists deny (v. 22). Since it is the 'last hour', John wants his readers to be on their guard against that which is false and to remain true to that which is true.

When it comes to the secessionists themselves, there are three things that we can learn from this passage. First, they are indeed secessionists, for as John says in 2:19 'they went out from us' (NIV and KJV), thus demonstrating that 'they did not really belong to us'. In this context, the 'us' refers to the Christian community to whom John has written and with whom he shares a common gospel commitment. As one whose gospel proclamation about Jesus the Christ drew the readers into true fellowship with God (1:3,4), John is himself in fellowship with the community. Thus when the secessionists break fellowship with the community, they break fellowship with John.

This breach in fellowship with John and with the community is, however, no small thing for it arises from fundamental doctrinal disagreement. For John and for the community, the basis of fellowship with God and with each other is the truth about Jesus, particularly the truth that the man Jesus was and is indeed the Christ of God. As we saw earlier there can be no true fellowship with God without fellowship with His Son, Jesus Christ (1:3). The secessionists, however, deny that Jesus is the Christ or more literally, that the Christ is Jesus (v. 22). From their point of view, God's Christ could never be associated with the human Jesus, certainly not in his weakness and death. It is this denial which, secondly, constitutes them as *'anti-christs'*, that is, those who are opposed to the Christ, rather than the *pseudo-*or false-christs that Jesus warned against (see Mark 13:22), though, as we shall see, they were *pseudo* prophets (*cf* 4:1). John's clear and still highly relevant point is that one must not separate the Jesus of history from the Christ of faith. To do this, is to deny, not only the Son, but the Father as well (v. 23) and thus to demonstrate that one is a stranger to the truth.

The third characteristic of the secessionists is that they are deceivers, those who attempt to lead others astray (v. 26). And it is because of this attempt on the part of the secessionists to draw away disciples that John is so anxious not only to warn his readers but also to remind them of the truth which they 'heard from the beginning' (v. 24), truth to which they are to hold fast. It is striking that John describes this holding fast to the truth in terms of the truth 'remaining *in*' the believers (v. 24). The reason for this is the connection that exists between the 'truth' which was heard in the beginning and the 'anointing' that we received 'from the Holy One' (v. 20). The result of having received this 'anointing' is that the readers 'know the truth' (v. 20) in particular the truth about Jesus (v. 22).

This close connection between the 'anointing' and the 'truth' in this paragraph corresponds to the connection between the Holy Spirit and the truth found later in the letter (see 3:24–4:6). Thus it seems reasonable that the word 'anointing' in this passage is in fact a reference to the Holy Spirit who indwells *all* believers with the result that *all* believers 'know the truth' (v. 20).

But why not simply refer to the Spirit as John does elsewhere in the letter? The answer is surely to be found in the play on words between 'anointing' and 'Christ' (Anointed One). In contrast to the secessionists who may well have claimed a sacred anointing not available to all, those who are truly anointed by God and who truly have His Spirit within them are the ones who all believe and hold firm to the truth about the Anointed One. Those who deny the truth that Jesus is the Christ are not real, but counterfeit (v. 27), denying the Father because they deny the Son (v. 23). On the other hand, those who acknowledge Jesus the Son and remain in Jesus the Son (v. 24) are the ones who are truly anointed by the Father and who know both the Father and the Son. It is this knowledge, as John tells us elsewhere (John 17:3), which is the promised eternal life (v. 25).

From text to message

As we noted above, 1 John 2:18-27 brings us face to face with the historical situation underlying the letter for the first time. This does not mean however that in teaching this passage we simply adopt a descriptive approach. While it is true that John has a particular group of false teachers in mind, it is clear from John's own words that the conduct and teaching of these men is typical of what we can expect in 'the last hour'. We should therefore expect to find such divisive conduct and deceptive teaching within the nominal church today as indeed we do. As in John's day, so the church today needs to be warned against those who embody the spirit of 'antichrist'.

The passage also speaks very powerfully into the relativistic and pluralistic culture of our day. It gives us a clear opportunity to affirm two great evangelical truths. First, it reminds us that there is indeed only one way to the Father and that is through His Son, Jesus Christ. Verse 23 is of vital importance in this regard – 'No one who denies the Son has the Father; whoever acknowledges the Son has the Father'. Second, the passage reminds us of the reality and importance of what an earlier generation of evangelicals called *the right of private judgement* in all matters of faith. Verses 24-27 remind every believer that the apostolic gospel and the indwelling Holy Spirit are all that the believer needs for a real and growing relationship with God. It is not that John denies the value of teaching for believers or he would not have written a letter filled with teaching. But he does deny the priestly role claimed by some teachers and urges all believers to weigh all that they hear in the light of scripture and with the discernment that comes from the Spirit of God.

Getting the message clear: the theme

- All who acknowledge that Jesus is the Christ are the true 'anointed ones', knowing both the Father and the Son and thus enjoying eternal life. Those who deny that Jesus is the Christ are not 'anointed ones' but antichrists, knowing neither the Father nor the Son and thus strangers to the eternal life of God which is ours only by acknowledging *both* the Father *and* Jesus the Son.

- The Apostolic gospel and indwelling Spirit of God give to believers all that they need for a real and growing relationship with the Father through His Son Jesus Christ. Every believer is to weigh what they hear against this gospel and with the discernment given by the Sprit.

Getting the message clear: the aim

To encourage those who believe that Jesus is the Christ to remain true to that faith, even when it is undermined by those who claim to speak for God.

A way in

Given current scepticism about the person of Jesus and the various attempts to redefine Jesus in our own terms, this passage presents us with a great opportunity to speak about the vital link that exists between history and faith, and more particularly between the Christ of faith and the Jesus of history. Modern spirituality claims that it is possible to know God through an act of sincere faith or spiritual encounter, independent of a personal faith in the man Jesus Christ. This approach to spirituality is by no means a new thing, but it is as misguided today as it was when John first wrote his letter. For John, as for the whole of the New Testament, relationship with God is, however, only possible through faith in Jesus the Christ. It is only as we acknowledge that Jesus is the Christ and put our trust in Him that we can be said to truly acknowledge the Father.

Another way in is to focus on John's play on the words 'Christ' (Anointed One) and 'anointing'. The latter word speaks of spirituality and the insight given by the Holy Spirit. Such insight is of vital importance for a relationship with God. What is striking is that a true spirituality must of necessity involve a true Christology, a Christology which identifies the Jesus of history and thus of the New Testament scriptures with the Christ of God.

Ideas for application

- The way to eternal life is to be found only in the knowledge of Jesus Christ, the true Son of God. To acknowledge the Son is to acknowledge the Father; to deny the Son is to deny the Father and to forfeit the life which the Father gives.

- All true believers have the witness of the Holy Spirit (the anointing) within their hearts. As elsewhere in the New Testament, the hallmark of those who possess the Spirit is that they acknowledge Jesus as God's Anointed One, the Son of God.

- Authentic faith in Jesus will from time to time be tested by those who present a different way to God. Such teaching which divides the Christ of faith and the Jesus of history will in effect also divide the church. True doctrine unites the church; false doctrine divides.

- Despite the sophistication of so-called 'new spiritualties' the ordinary believer in Jesus has all that he or she needs to resist the deceptive words of false teachers and to stand firm in the faith. All true believers possess two great gifts, namely the historic gospel of Jesus Christ and the gift of the indwelling Holy Spirit of God who bears witness to the truth about Jesus. In the light of these gifts from God we are called to remain in the truth.

Suggestions for preaching

Sermon

False or True? (1 John 2:18-27)

1. Introduction – Many ways to God?
    - A confused world
    - A Divided church
    - A Sign of the times
2. The Fundamental Error
    - An *ahistorical* Christ
    - An *ahistorical* Gospel
    - Jesus-less Christianity
3. The Way of Truth
    - What was heard from the beginning
    - Jesus, the Son of the Father
    - The Spirit, the Anointing of the Holy One
4. The Way of Life
    - True to Father and Son
    - Firm in the Gospel
    - Confident in the Spirit and the Truth

Suggestions for teaching

Questions to help understand the passage

1. To whom is John referring when he uses the address 'dear children'?
2. What does John mean by the phrase 'the last hour'?
3. What in particular characterises the 'last hour' according to this passage?
4. What are the characteristics of those to whom John refers as 'antichrists'?
5. What, by contrast, characterises the 'dear children'?
6. To whom or what does the phrase 'the anointing' refer?
7. To what does the phrase 'what you have heard from the beginning' refer?
8. What does John exhort his readers to do in the light of the teaching of the antichrists?

Questions to help apply the passage

1. What does this passage teach us about the presence and prevalence of false teaching in the world and within the nominal church?
2. What are some of the ways in which false teaching manifests today?
3. What resources do believers have to withstand false teaching?
4. In what way does this passage encourage believers to stand firm in the faith?

5. In what way does this passage enable us to answer those who claim that there are many ways to God?
6. How does this passage underline that Christianity is a historical faith?
7. According to this passage, what is the hallmark of the man or woman who is indwelt by the Spirit of God?

6
Children of God
(1 John 2:28–3:10)

Introduction

That the question of sin in the life of the true believer is a vexed, yet vitally important one need hardly be stated. That it is one about which there is often a great deal of misunderstanding and thus the potential for deception is painfully true, not only from experience, but also from texts such as 1 John 2:28–3:10. The question of the believer's attitude to sin had, of course, been raised by John earlier in the letter, as we saw in our discussion of 1 John 1:5–2:2. In 1 John 2:28–3:10, John returns to the subject, and the context, as in the earlier passage, is once again the false, but confident and thus potentially misleading, claims of the secessionists. As the exhortation in 3:7 makes clear, John is particularly concerned that his readers avoid being 'led astray' by teaching which claims that those who 'know God' and especially those who speak for God are above the ordinary disciplines of righteous living. At the same time John is well aware that the best form of defence against such error is the pursuit of what is true, not merely in terms of truth believed (as in 2:18-27), but also in terms of truth lived out in practice. Thus the paragraph begins with an urgent appeal to 'continue (*lit.* remain) in him' (i.e. Christ) until the day of His return (2:28).

As we shall see, the passage builds carefully on what has gone before. But it also introduces key truths that are of vital importance for the rest of the letter. Most important among these are the fact that all true believers have been 'born of God' (2:29, 3:9) and thus are 'children of God' (3:1,2,10) and the fact that every believer can and should have 'confidence' before God, both in a daily relationship with the Lord (see 3:21; 5:14), but also on the approaching Day of the Lord (2:28, *cf* 4:17).

Listening to the text

Context and structure

At first glance, 1 John 2:28 appears to be nothing more than a repetition of the previous verse – a heartfelt appeal to resist the deceitful words of the secessionists and to persevere in the truth which was received from the beginning. On closer examination, however, it is clear that although the exhortation to persevere is repeated, both the motive for and the nature of the perseverance differ in 2:24-27 and 2:28-29. First, in 2:24-27, John exhorts his readers to persevere in *belief of the truth* about Jesus whereas in 2:28-29, he exhorts his readers to persevere in *doing what is right*. Second, in 2:24-27 the motive for perseverance in the faith is the 'anointing' which they all received from the Father, i.e. the Holy Spirit. In 2:28-29 the motive for persevering in doing what is right is the righteous character of God the Father (2:29; *cf* 3:7) and the 'appearance' of Jesus, both in history (3:5,8) and at the end of the age (2:28; 3:2). The appeals for perseverance in 2:27 and 2:28 are thus complementary rather than identical and together they reinforce the fundamental truth that authentic Christianity is a matter of *both* doctrine *and* life, a truth which was denied by at least some of the secessionists.

The sub-division of the paragraph is not straightforward and two possibilities can be suggested. First, focussing on John's twin exhortations to his readers ('remain in him' (2:28 NLT) and 'do not be led astray' (3:7)), the paragraph can be divided into two parts, namely 2:28-3:6 and 3:7-10. Alternatively, focussing on the two 'appearances' of the Lord, His appearance at the end of the age (2:28;3:3) and His appearance in history (3:5;8), the passage can be divided into two parts, namely 2:28–3:3 and 3:4-10. In both subdivisions there is an emphasis upon the righteousness of God the Father and the Christ, the Son of God and upon the necessity for righteousness among all who claim to be born of God and to be children of God (2:29; 3:7,9-10). In both subdivisions John's objective is the same, namely to encourage (2:28) and to warn (3:7) his readers.

Finally, we note that although there is a transition in 3:10 from righteous living to a life of love toward fellow believers, the primary subject of 3:11-24, the declaration 'this is the message you have heard from the beginning' (3:11) in fact marks the beginning of a new section. As in 2:17 and 2:27, 3:10 thus functions both as a conclusion to the present paragraph and a bridge into the next.

Working through the text

An Urgent Appeal (2:28–3:4)

As noted above, the passage begins with an emphatic address and an urgent appeal. The 'now' of 2:28, recalls the 'now' of 2:18, a reminder to John's readers that they are living in the 'last hour', the time of the antichrists and their deceptive teaching (*cf* 4:3). It also anticipates the 'now' of 3:2, the 'now' of the readers' present privilege and experience as 'children of God'. The familiar phrase 'dear children' again reinforces John's close pastoral relationship with his readers and serves as an added incentive for them to heed the appeal to 'continue in him' (2:28). This appeal to 'continue' or to 'remain' in Christ must be taken to heart by the readers, particularly in the light of the future 'appearing' or 'coming' of Christ. The belief that this coming of the Lord will indeed take place is assumed by John on behalf of his readers, but it may well have been questioned by the secessionists with their emphasis on present salvation through knowledge.

John's point is simple and compelling. Those who do in fact believe that the Lord will return will surely want to be prepared for that event. To be prepared, in John's terms, is to be 'confident and unashamed'. 'Confidence' is an important word in the second part of 1 John. It is used in two ways. In 3:21 and 5:14 it is used to describe present 'confidence' before the Lord in prayer. But in 2:28 and 4:17, the word is used with reference to confidence before the Lord on the day of His return. The use of the word in 2:28 in apposition to 'unashamed' (used only in 2:28), suggests that in 2:28 and in 4:17 the word 'confidence' refers to the sure grounds of acceptance before Christ, rather than subjective feelings of confidence. Because Christ is the Righteous One (2:1), the One who on the basis of his atoning death (2:2) forgives sin and cleanses from all unrighteousness (1:9), it follows that those who 'remain in Him' can be both 'confident and unashamed before him at his coming' (2:28). Consequently, it also then follows that those who want this confidence must of necessity remain in Him.

In 2:29, the focus shifts from the return of Christ the Righteous One, to God the Father whom the believers 'know' to be 'righteous'. All who are in Christ are in Him because they have been 'born of God' (*cf* 3:9; 4:7; 5:1,4,18). It is for this reason that John can call them 'children of God', not in the presumptuous way of the false teachers, but in a way that recognizes God's lavish act of love (3:1) in Christ to those who are undeserving. It is this loving act of regeneration which enabled the believers to 'know him' (i.e. Christ) in contrast to the world (and the false teachers) who 'did not know him' (3:1). And it is this act of knowing Christ and continuing in him which thus marks the believers out as different from the world. Unknown and unacknowledged by the world, the believers nevertheless have the great privilege of actually being the children of God (note John's declaration in 3:1 – 'and this is what we are!').

However, since God is righteous, it must surely follow that all who are 'born of him' will make every effort to do 'what is right' (2:29). Thus doing what is right, while not the only evidence of being born of God is nevertheless a necessary characteristic of all who claim the privilege to call God Father. This is John's point when he states that 'everyone who does what is right has been born of him'. He is not prescribing a way to be 'born of God', but describing one way by which the validity of such claims to have been 'born of God' may be evaluated. For those, who for all their failings, do pursue righteousness in recognition of the righteousness of God their Father and the righteousness of Jesus their Lord, this pursuit of righteousness becomes both the way to continue in Christ (2:28) and the way to build true assurance in the face of the unsettling but spurious claims of the false teachers.

This recognition of the pursuit of righteousness as one building block for true assurance is of the utmost importance, given the reality of the believer's daily experience in the world. All believers look forward with certain 'hope' (3:3) to the future appearance of the Lord. And knowing that the Lord who will return is 'pure', we have the added hope that 'when he appears, we will be like him, for we shall see him as he is' (3:2). The return of the Lord will thus bring to fulfilment the sanctifying work begun at regeneration! This recognition and hope is of great comfort to all who look forward to his coming.

But the reality is that in this life believers are not yet what they will be when Jesus returns. In John's play on words in 3:2, 'though we are now children of God what we will be then, when he appears, has not yet now appeared'. Here then, is the classic 'now' and 'not yet' of the every disciple's experience. And herein lies the importance of, first, the assurance that all who remain in him, though not yet pure as he is pure, are indeed God's children and, second, the earlier reminder that all who sin may approach Jesus for forgiveness and purification (1:9). In the light of what Christ has done to make atonement for sins, and in the light of his coming and his transforming power, believers, while not yet pure, have every incentive to 'purify [themselves] just as he is pure' (3:3). Indeed, they not only have every incentive to do what is right, but according to John, they also have an obligation to do so. The expectation is that everyone who is in Christ and looks for his return with all that it means, will of necessity desire purity and make every effort to keep pursuing what is right.

An Urgent Warning (3:4-10)

In 3:4-10, the focus shifts from the believers, with their privilege and moral obligation as the children of God, to the antichrists and their efforts to lead John's readers astray (3:7). What is striking is the fact that John's focus in this passage is not on the content of the secessionists' teaching, but on the personal moral failure of these men and their lack of righteousness in daily life.

The passage begins with an absolute and unambiguous declaration, both about sinners and sin. Without exception, says John, 'everyone who sins breaks the law' (*lit.* does lawlessness) (3:4). Although this is true of all sinners, one must ask who in particular John has in mind when he makes this declaration. Comparing 3:4a with 2:29b, we note that the clause 'everyone who sins' is in antithesis to the clause 'everyone who does what is right'. Since we know from 2:29 that this latter clause refers to those who have been born of God, we might expect 3:4 to read 'everyone who sins has not been born of God'. Indeed, in 3:10, John does in fact say something very close to this when he declares that anyone who 'does not do what is right is not God's child'. However, the declaration in 3:4 that 'everyone who sins breaks the law' is followed by a second declaration that 'sin is lawlessness'. And it is this second declaration that provides the clue to who John has in mind with these words and what his purpose is in this passage.

The key here is to note the connection between this sin which is 'lawlessness' and John's earlier declaration that 'the last hour' had in fact dawned (2:18). As we noted above, the eschatological focus of 2:18 is maintained in 2:28–3:3. The dawning of the 'last hour' means that the Lord will appear (2:28). But as John's readers know all too well, the Lord who will appear in the future has appeared in the past with a very specific purpose in mind, namely to 'take away our sins' (3:5; *cf* 1:8–2:2) and 'to destroy the devil's work' (3:8). Here, then, is the fundamental conflict of the 'last hour' – the conflict between the righteous Son of God (3:7) and the devil who 'has been sinning from the beginning'(3:8).

Earlier in the letter (2:2), John has already made clear that the conflict between Jesus the Son of God and the evil one had been resolved decisively in favour of Jesus and His people. It is for this reason that those whose 'sins have been forgiven on account of his name' (2:12) can be said to have 'overcome the evil one' (2:13). Furthermore, as 3:2 declares, this victory by Jesus for and in His people will be brought to triumphant completion at His return. In the end then, both the children of God and the Son of God will stand victorious.

In the interim, however, and for the duration of the 'last hour', the conflict between the Son of God and the devil spills over into the lives of the children of God, not only in their struggle against sin (3:5) and the pursuit of 'righteousness' but also in their struggle with the children of the devil (3:10). Those who are born of God and in whom God's seed remains (3:9), while not sinless, will strive against sin because they are characterised not by lawlessness which characterised their former way of life but by a new desire for righteousness. Those who are the children of the devil will, like their father the devil, be given over to the sin which is 'lawlessness' (3:4,8). And this 'lawlessness' which is a characteristic of the devil's children in the 'last hour' will manifest itself in two closely connected ways: first, in the spirit of antichrist, in opposition to the Christ and His righteous purposes (antichrist–2:18); second, in opposition to the children of God particularly by trying to lead them astray (3:7). This suggests that the sinners or lawless ones of whom John has in mind in 3:4-10 are neither sinners in general, nor believers in their struggle against sin, but the antichrists of 2:18, the false teachers whose deceptive words must be rejected on the basis of their lawless and thus inevitably loveless lives (3:10). In 1 John, as elsewhere in the rest of the New Testament, lawlessness and a lack of love for Christ and His people are closely connected and false prophets are known by their fruits!

From text to message

Given the exegetical and theological complexity of the passage, it is, perhaps, easy to fall into one of two errors when teaching 1 John 2:28–3:10. On the one hand, we may be tempted to gloss over the passage and to preach our theological framework, thus failing to show our hearers how the passage itself makes the points which we want to make. On the other hand and in a genuine attempt to let the passage speak, we may find ourselves and our hearers bogged down in the detail of the text and so end up missing the expository wood for the exegetical trees. Thus as we approach what is a difficult passage, we are reminded both of the necessity of hard work in the study and of the importance of weighing carefully which work is to be brought to the pulpit and which is to be left behind closed doors. And here, perhaps, more than anywhere, we will benefit from a clear statement of the theme and aim of the passage as a guide for exposition.

Given the length and complexity of the passage, at least two talks will be required to do justice to its message. The first talk (1 John 2:28–3:3) could then focus on the privilege that believers have to be called the children of God by virtue of Divine regeneration and the hope of full salvation that will be ours when Christ returns. Both of these, the privilege and the hope, should thus be an incentive for us to continue in Christ daily by pursuing righteousness. The second talk (1 John 3:4-10) could underline the fact that no one is exempt from the call to a righteous life, least of all those who speak for God. Word and deed, doctrine and life must always go together. The fact that preachers are sinners does of course mean that there will be a gap between what we preach and how we live. In this passage John reminds us, however, that it is a gap with which we should never be at ease.

Getting the message clear: the theme

- Those who are truly born of God and who look forward to Christ's return will prepare for that return by pursuing righteousness. This is the appropriate and necessary response of all believers to God's love and kindness in making us part of His family.
- The best antidote to false teaching is perseverance in what is true and right. All believers are called to continue in Christ by persevering in righteousness of life.
- False doctrine will inevitably lead to moral failure, both in those who follow false doctrine and in those who teach it. Teaching should always be tested both by content and consequent way of life.
- Our status as children of God is as a result of God's undeserved love. Such a privileged status will

inevitably lead to conflict with those who do not know God.

Getting the message clear: the aim

- To urge believers to continue in Christ by saying no to sin and yes to what is right.
- To warn believers against false teaching and to urge them to test what they hear against the way of life of those who teach.

A way in

One way in to talk 1 would be to begin by speaking about the link that exists between privilege and the responsibility to live up to the privilege that is ours. This is true in all of life and it is no less true when it comes to the Christian life. The New Testament describes the privileges that all believers enjoy in a rich variety of ways. In our passage, in particular, we are reminded that all believers enjoy the present status of children of God and the future hope of Christlikeness when the Lord returns. It is these privileges that motivate us to continue in Christ and to persevere in righteousness of life.

Another way in to talk 1 would be to speak about the struggle that all believers have with sin in their daily lives. What we are now can often be a discouragement to us. Sometimes this sense of failure can make us want to throw in the towel and to stop struggling against sin. When we look at our track record there is often precious little to motivate us. The passage before us has a very different perspective both of our present status before God and of our future. And as our perspective is changed we find a new motivation not to give in but to persevere to the end.

One way in to talk 2 would be to remind our hearers that the Christian life involves a battle, a battle in which we all must choose a side. Fundamentally this battle was fought and won by the Lord during his life, death and resurrection. As John reminds us, the Son of God appeared to take away our sins and to destroy the work of the devil. But the battle that was joined and won by Christ is still in evidence today – waged against the children of God by the children of the devil, in particular the false teachers who promote the devil's lies. These lies, crafty in their design and deadly in their intention, seek to underplay the seriousness of sin, in teacher and hearer alike. In the passage before us, John exposes the lie for what it is and encourages his hearers to stand firm in the battle for truth and righteousness.

Ideas for application

- The idea of confidence before the Lord on the day of judgement is a striking one, one which many who do not understand the gospel misconstrue for arrogance. Such confidence is a precious thing however and the possibility of such confidence provides a great opportunity for a gospel conversation.
- All Christians struggle with the fact that we still fall short of what we want to be and what we will be when the Lord returns. At times the struggle seems too much for us, especially if it comes to some besetting sin. The devil would want believers to capitulate and to give up the fight for righteousness. What we are now by God's grace (regenerated

children of God) and what we will be when Christ returns (made like Him) should motivate us to keep on going, no matter how tough the fight is.

- Personal godliness will not be a reality without personal effort on the part of the believer.
- The pursuit of godliness is a necessary evidence of being a child of God.
- The church has always been and will always be troubled by those who claim that their spiritual status exempts them from the need for personal godliness.
- The devil, opposed as he is to Jesus' purposes in the world and in the life of the believer, will endeavour to trip believers up in their walk with God. False teaching is one of the tools that the devil uses to this end.
- Jesus came to deal with sin and thus destroy the work of the devil. This fact should motivate believers to be ruthless with sin in their own lives.

Suggestions for preaching

Sermon 1

The Way of Truth (1 John 2:28–3:3)

1. Introduction – Concerning Privilege and Responsibility
2. Our Present Status
    - Beloved Children of God
    - Unknown by the World

- Not yet what we will be

3. Our Future Hope

- Confident and unashamed
- Made like Him

4. Our Present Responsibility

- Continue in Him
- Purify yourself

Sermon 2
Don't buy the Lie (1 John 3:4-10)

1. Introduction – Big claims, Empty words

- What the false teachers claimed
- What the false teachers missed

2. The Truth about sin

- Sin is lawlessness
- Sin needs to be opposed

3. The mission of Jesus

- To take away sin
- To destroy the devil's work

4. Mind the Gap – Life and Doctrine

- By their fruits you will know them
- Don't buy the lie

Suggestions for teaching

Questions to help understand the passage

1. What does it mean in this context to 'continue in Christ'?
2. Why should believers be concerned to continue in Christ?
3. To whom do the pronouns 'He' and 'Him' refer in 2:29?
4. On what basis can believers be said to be 'children of God'?
5. What is true of the Christ with respect to sin?
6. What is true of us with respect to sin?
7. What will be true of us when He appears?
8. How will this come about?
9. How is sin defined in this passage?
10. What does this definition of sin tell us about the attitude of the false teachers?
11. Why did Christ 'appear'?
12. How should Christ's mission shape our belief and teaching about sin?
13. What is one important mark of the true teacher?
14. What is one characteristic of the false teacher?

Questions to help apply the passage

1. What privilege do believers have in the present?

2. What hope do believers have for the future?
3. What is the relationship between privilege and responsibility in the Christian life?
4. How does this relationship work out in terms of personal godliness?
5. What place does personal effort and choice play in our growth in godliness?
6. Why is perseverance as a Christian important?
7. What are the things that hinder us from persevering as we should?
8. What does this passage teach about the need for discernment?
9. What standard does it give us by which to evaluate those who claim to speak for God?
10. How would you summarise the daily life of the believer in relation to sin and godliness?
11. Why should every Christian engage in a daily battle against sin?
12. How does the daily fight against sin strengthen assurance?

7
The Gospel of Love (1 John 3:11-24)

Introduction

The theme of love for the brothers with which the previous section ended (3:10b) and to which John had already referred earlier in the letter (2:9-11), is now brought into primary focus. Once again it is love for the brothers as evidence of an authentic relationship with God that is in view. From the very beginning, the Christians to whom John was writing had been taught to obey the 'new' command of Jesus, namely, that they 'should love one another' (3:11, 23; *cf* 2:7-11). This command was not, however, a substitute for belief in Jesus but, as 3:23 makes clear, a necessary companion of saving faith. It is this link between belief in Jesus and love for others who believe in Jesus that gives such love its evidential status.

But for love to function as evidence of saving faith and of an authentic relationship with God, it must, of course, itself be tested and authenticated. It is with this in mind that John sets criteria so that we may 'know what love is' (3:16). True love for the brothers will be love modelled on the love of Christ for His people, sacrificial love in action, rather than a love which is all talk. As with their other bold but spurious claims to reality, this love 'with words and speech' only (3:18) was in all likelihood the 'love' which John saw as characteristic of the secessionists. Certainly actions which divided the community or teaching which undermined the confidence before God of those who trusted in Christ could hardly be described as loving! In marked contrast to this, sacrificial and practical love, especially to those who were unable to reciprocate, was (and still is) the true mark of the Christian, an evidence that one belongs to the truth, enjoys an intimate relationship with God, sealed by His indwelling Spirit (3:24).

Listening to the text

Context and structure

As noted earlier, 2:18–3:10 ends with the statement 'anyone who does not do what is right is not God's child nor is anyone who does not love his brother or sister' (3:10). Doing what is right and showing love to fellow believers are thus both identified as necessary characteristics of all who have been 'born of God'. Given that the emphasis throughout 2:18–3:10 is primarily on the first part of this statement, i.e. doing what is right, and given the importance of brotherly love as one of the distinguishing marks of the true believer, it is thus to be expected that the main focus of the following passage (3:11-24) would be on love for the brothers. And this is precisely what we find. This confirms that 3:10 is indeed a bridging verse, summarising what has gone before and introducing a new, but closely connected discussion about the importance and nature of love for the brothers.

The passage can be divided into three sub-sections. The first sub-section (3:11-15), begins with the words 'This is the message...' and consists of two parts. First, there is an urgent appeal to the believers not to mimic that hatred of righteousness which is so characteristic of the world and the devil. Second, there is a word of affirmation, a reinforcement of the fact that love for the brothers is indeed evidence of having passed from death to life. The second sub-section (3:16-18), begins with the words 'This is how we know...' The purpose of this section is to define that love which is indeed the characteristic of the true believer. True love or 'love in truth' as John prefers to call it (3:18) finds both its pattern and its motivation in the love that Christ showed in His death for His people. By defining true love in this way, John thus provides yet another means by which his readers can both evaluate the claims of the secessionists and cultivate a true sense of confidence before the Lord.

The third and final sub-section (3:19-24) both begins and ends with the words 'This is how we know.' The focus of these statements is the assurance and confidence of the believer and in each case they point forward to the basis of such assured knowledge. Believers can know and indeed will know (the verb is future in 3:19) that they 'belong to the truth' because they practice love for the brothers and in this way are able *lit* 'to persuade their hearts' in the presence of the God who knows all hearts and is greater than all hearts. Believers can know God lives in them and they live in Him, by virtue of the God given gift of the Spirit who produces both faith in Christ and obedience to Christ's command to love. As in the previous paragraph, the final statement then also provides a bridge to the next section with its appeal to 'test the spirits' to see whether they are indeed from God.

Working through the text

For the second time in the letter, John begins a section with the words 'This is the message....' On the previous occasion (1 John 1:5), the phrase referred to the message which John and his associates 'heard from Him' (i.e. Christ) and 'declared to you' (i.e. the readers of the letter). At its heart, this message consisted of the declaration that 'God is light; in Him there is no darkness at all', a declaration which challenged John's readers to keep walking in the light themselves, but which also provided a standard by which the validity of claims to know God could be tested. In the present passage, the message is one which the readers have 'heard from the beginning', that is, from the beginning of their own experience of the Christian faith. One might expect that the content of the message would once again be a declaration about God, namely, that God is love. Such a declaration does in fact come later in the letter (4:8,16) and the truth that God is love is certainly presupposed in all that John says in the present paragraph, but it is not in fact the focus of the message. What was heard from the beginning was the message that believers in the Lord Jesus 'should love one another' (3:11).

John's use of the subjunctive implies obligation, hence the NIV's translation 'should'. As we shall see, John returns to this obligation at the end of the paragraph by referring to God's command to 'believe in the name of his Son, Jesus Christ and to love one another' (3:23). But for the moment he undergirds his appeal, not by reference to a Divine command, but by a vivid example drawn from Bible history. The example is the murder of Abel by his brother Cain, a murder which both identified Cain as one who belonged to the evil one rather than to God (3:12) and which showed a deep-seated hatred toward righteousness and therefore toward righteous deeds on the part of someone whose own deeds were evil (3:12). This connection between the evil one, evil deeds and the hatred of righteousness is important to note for it implies that hatred of righteousness will be a feature of all those who are children of the devil. And since a love for what is right and a love for the brothers is closely connected (3:10), it follows that a hatred of righteousness will spill over into a hatred of those who do what is right. Thus believers should not be surprised if the world, which 'is under the control of the evil one' (5:19), hates them (3:13). Such hatred of believers by those who belong to the evil one is a sign that the latter 'remain in death' (3:14,15). By contrast, love for the brothers is a clear sign that one has 'passed from death to life' (3:14). Love for the brothers is thus an important ground of assurance for believers.

In 3:16-18, John directs his readers' attention to a standard by which true love can be measured. If love for the brothers is to be used as a measure for what is true or false, it is essential that this love itself should be shown not to be counterfeit. John draws a striking contrast between Cain who hated his brother and murdered him and Jesus Christ 'who laid down His life for us' (3:16 NIV and KJV). True love is thus sacrificial and life-giving rather than life-taking. This love of Christ is both the standard by which true love is to be measured and a mandate that believers must follow. As the recipients of this love of God in Christ 'we ought to lay down our lives for our brothers and sisters' (3:16). Love with 'words or speech alone' is mere talk and easy to do; love with actions and in truth is the love that should be characteristic of those for whom Christ died (3:18). Such love finds expression in the everyday realities of life, such as practical care for those who are in material need (3:17). This is clearly an example of 'love with actions' (3:18). But it is also a clear example of love 'in truth' because it does not arise out of self-interest or a hope of recompense but out of 'the truth' which was heard from the beginning, that believers should exemplify the love of Christ to one another.

In 3:19-24, the focus shifts to the assurance that believers can and should have before the Lord, particularly with respect to prayer for help and grace in time of need. The fundamental problem that all believers face from time to time, is the problem of the exposure of their own hearts in the presence of the God who knows everything (3:20). On some occasions, our hearts do not in fact condemn us and we have full confidence in approaching God to ask for anything which is in keeping with His pleasure and will. This restriction on the word 'anything' while not explicitly stated is entirely appropriate in the context of a life lived seeking to obey the Lord and to please Him rather than self (3:22; *cf* 5:14).

But there are other times when the believer is very conscious of his or her failure to live in love or in obedience to God's goodwill, times at which our 'hearts condemn us' (3:20). At such times it is important to remember that God who knows all things and who in Christ has made a way for us to be His children is indeed greater than our hearts (3:20). But it is also necessary at such times to take action to 'set our hearts at rest' in the presence of God (3:19). John's original 'persuade our hearts' underlines the fact that at such times of personal doubt before God, it will be necessary for the believers to 'persuade' or 'reassure' their hearts that they do indeed 'belong to the truth' (3:19) and that they can approach God with confidence. But this persuasion cannot be on the basis of subjective feelings of confidence. It must be based upon the objective evidence of a changed life, in this case a life of love 'with actions and in truth' (3:18). A life of love 'in truth' is thus the way that 'we know that we belong to the truth'.

John's purpose in 3:11-24 has been to provide his 'dear children' and 'dear friends' with further evidence of an authentic relationship with God, namely love for the brothers. But such evidences are not to be viewed in isolation from each other and this point is made with particular clarity in 3:23-24. True assurance before the Lord is based upon four inter-related things: first, belief of the truth about Jesus (2:20-27) and thus belief in the name of Jesus (3:23); second, true love for fellow believers, brothers and sisters in Christ (2:9-11; 3:10-23); third, a commitment to doing what is right in obedience to God's commands (2:3-6; 2:29–3:10); fourth, the inner witness of the indwelling Spirit of God (2:20,27; 3:24). Each of these will appear again in the letter as John continues to assure those who believe in Jesus that they do indeed have eternal life (*cf* 5:13). But it is the witness of the indwelling Spirit of God in particular which occupies his attention in 4:1-6, the next section of the letter. Our present passage concludes with the statement: 'And this is how we know that he lives in us: we know it by the Spirit he gave us' (3:24). This is true but it raises a key question, namely, how can claims to possess the Spirit or to speak by the authority of the Spirit be tested? It is this key question that John addresses in 4:1-6.

From text to message

There could hardly be a clearer example of the radical difference between the way of the world and authentic Christianity than 1 John 3:11-24. In contrast to the world's default definition of love as sentimentality and/or romance,

1 John 3:11-24 provides a robust definition of true love as sacrificial service for the good of another, even when such service is undeserved. In contrast to the subjective and mystical approach of the world to spirituality and the misguided notion that doubt is the true expression of humility, 1 John 3:11-24 speaks about the knowledge of God in terms that are personal without being individualistic, assured without being presumptuous. It is an encouraging but also a challenging passage, one that requires careful thought, especially in regard to the interpretation of 3:19-22 which is not straightforward.

The passage is probably best taught in two or possibly three parts. In talk 1, based on 3:11-18, the focus would be on love for the brothers as one of the evidences of true Christian experience, taking the time to clarify precisely what is meant when one speaks about love. Here the contrast between Cain and Jesus is important. It is also important not to lose sight of the central point of the passage expressed in 3:14 –'we know that we have passed from death to life because…' We should thus take care not to get sidetracked into speaking about the need for practical love and generosity (important though this is), but rather to keep the focus on the theme of assurance and the role that such sacrificial love with actions rather than mere words plays in our having such assurance before God.

In talk 2, based on 3:19-24, the focus would again be on assurance, but now the emphasis would be on how our own hearts can undermine such assurance given our own poor track record. Of course, one does not always feel a lack of confidence before the Lord and here it is worth noting that commitment to obedience and a life that pleases the Lord is a real boost to one's confidence in prayer. But given that we are sinners such times of confidence can easily give way to times of real doubt and uncertainty. This is an experience with which most of us will be able to identify. John's counsel regarding what we should do about the 'condemning heart' and his reminder that God who is all-knowing is greater than our hearts is thus invaluable.

In talk 3, based on 3:23-24, one could underline the important truth that Christian assurance is a multifaceted reality and, as we saw above, is based on a number of closely related things. The link between belief in Christ, love for the brothers, obedience to God's commands and the inner witness of the Holy Spirit could thus be explored for the first time. Here care must be taken to explore such a link in the light of what has already been said in the letter and not to run ahead.

Getting the message clear: the theme

Authentic love for the brothers, modelled on the sacrificial love of Jesus, is an important and a vital foundation for assurance in one's relationship with God and confidence in one's approach to God. Such assurance, while personal and subjective, and while also a fruit of the Spirit's work in the heart of the believer, is always based on objective criteria. It is this fact which forms the key difference between true assurance and vain presumption.

Getting the message clear: the aim

- To encourage those who exhibit Christ-like love for their fellow believers that such love, though imperfect, is a sign that they have indeed passed from death to life.
- To encourage believers to approach God in prayer with confidence, notwithstanding the fact that

we sometimes feel unworthy of entering His presence.

A way in

One way in to talk 1 would be to begin by talking about the world's misconceptions about love and spirituality. Romance, sentiment, individualism and mysticism – these are what most people in the world mean when love for others or a relationship with the Divine are discussed. And, of course, our misconceptions about what love is are also then imported into our ideas of what God's love is like. It is, of course, quite correct to say, as many would say, that love matters when it comes to speaking about our relationship with God and with others. But it is also important to be clear about what true love is and about why such love with respect to fellow believers is so important in the case of our passage, as a key element of assurance and confidence before God.

One way in to talk 2 would be to begin by speaking about why confidence in God's presence is of the utmost importance especially when it comes to prayer. It is not that our confidence makes God any more disposed to hear, for He is gracious and kind even when we are full of doubts. But confidence with respect to our relationship with God does encourage us to be more prayerful. And that is a great thing. All of us, however, face a challenge when it comes to having confidence before the Lord for doubts that arise from time to time in our hearts. In 1 John 3:11-22, John addresses this challenge and provides a way to approach God with renewed confidence.

One way in to talk 3 is to begin by talking about the importance of assurance (as has been said before in the series!).

But it is also important not to be simplistic or reductionistic when it comes to assurance. Assurance is a multifaceted reality and this fact, underlying all of John's teaching in this letter, is made abundantly clear in 1 John 3:23-24. The passage thus gives us a key summary of what assurance is and how this assurance can be ours.

Ideas for application

- Brotherly love is and always has been one of the marks of the True Christian.
- True Christian love will always have the love of Jesus Christ as its motivation and model.
- Christ-like love is always practical and sacrificial.
- Love for our fellow believers and a love for righteousness are not mutually exclusive but complimentary. Love for righteousness will lead to a love of those who pursue what is right.
- There are times when every believer will feel doubt about our acceptance before God. At such times it is important to remember the grace of the God who is greater than our hearts. But it is also important to reassure our hearts in the light of actions done out of Christ-like love.
- God answers the prayers of His people.
- True assurance is a blend of the subjective and the objective. It is based upon the witness of the Spirit, faith in Jesus, love for our fellow believers and a desire to obey the Lord.

Suggestions for preaching

Sermon 1
The Way of Love (1 John 3:11-18)

1. Introduction – More than a feeling
2. The Mark of the Christian (3:11-15)
   - The message you heard...
   - The way of death
   - Surprising hate?
   - The way of life
3. Love is... (3:16-18)
   - The Model of Love
   - Love in action
   - Love in truth

Sermon 2
Confidence before God (1 John 3:19-22)

1. Introduction – Bold I approach?
   - The confidence we all need
   - The struggle we all face
2. Dealing with the heart
   - A reassured heart
   - A God who is greater

3. Confidence before God

    - Anything we ask?
    - All that we need!

Sermon 3

This is how we know… (1 John 3:23-24)

1. Introduction – Assurance or presumption?
2. Building blocks of assurance
    - Faith in Jesus
    - Love for the brothers
    - Keeping His commands
    - The witness of the Spirit
3. Alive in God

Suggestions for teaching

Questions to help understand the passage

1. What does John mean by the phrase 'from the beginning'?
2. What are the three key things about Cain that John highlights?
3. Why should believers not be surprised by the hatred of the world?
4. How do believers know that they have passed from death to life?

5. Why are hatred and the possession of eternal life mutually exclusive?
6. In what way does Jesus' love define true love?
7. What obligation does Christ's love place upon believers?
8. What is the difference between true and false love?
9. Why can Christians be confident in God's presence?
10. What does this passage teach us about dealing with doubt?
11. What are the four building blocks of true assurance?

Questions to help apply the passage

1. How would you describe the spiritual status of the true Christian from this passage?
2. Why is it important for Christians to love one another?
3. In what way does brotherly love encourage:
    - The one who loves?
    - Those who are loved?
4. What does it mean for us to love 'with actions and in truth'?
5. Why is it important to base such love on Christ's love for us?
6. What are some of the ways in which our hearts condemn us?

7. Where should we turn in times of doubt and uncertainty?
8. Why can we be confident that God will hear and answer our prayers?
9. What can we pray about as believers?
10. What safeguards our prayers from becoming self-centred?
11. How can we know for certain that we are in a true relationship with God?

8

A Call for Discernment (1 John 4:1-6)

Introduction

Despite its comparative brevity, 1 John 4:1-6 is in fact one of the most important passages in the letter. The repeated use of the word 'world' (six times in six verses) ties the passage firmly into the main theme of the second half of the letter as introduced in 2:15 (*see above*). Likewise the use of words such as 'truth' and 'falsehood' (4:6) and the references to the antichrists and false prophets who 'have gone out into the world' (4:1) show that this passage is closely aligned with 2:18-27 and is thus of key importance in confronting the actual danger facing John's readers.

In customary fashion, John addresses his readers as dear friends (*lit* beloved ones – 4:1 *cf* 2:7; 3:2,21; 4:7,11) and dear children (4:4 *cf* 2:1,12,28; 3:7,18: 5:21), thus calling to mind both his own personal and affectionate relationship with them and their own personal and privileged relationship with the Lord. In this way he builds a strong foundation for the appeal for spiritual discernment which follows. As we noted above, the context for this appeal is the destructive and divisive influence of the secessionists whom John now describes as false prophets (4:1), men who claim to speak by the Spirit of God but who in fact speak by the spirt of falsehood (4:6). In the midst of this appeal there is also an empowering affirmation, namely, a reminder of the great privilege that believers have thanks to the Spirit of Truth (4:4) who comes 'from God' and who dwells within them (4:1; *cf* 3:24) and of the victory that is already theirs by the power of the Spirit and in union with Christ.

Listening to the text

Context and structure

In 3:24, John reminded his readers that the gift of God's indwelling Spirit enables all believers to know that God lives in them. In 4:1-6, he appeals to them to exercise spiritual discernment. This discernment is made possible because the Spirit of God who indwells them is 'the Spirit of truth' (4:6). This appeal for spiritual discernment is necessitated by the presence of 'false prophets' who have 'gone out into the world' (4:1). It is expressed both in negative and positive terms (4:1) and leads directly to two statements in which John provides the criteria by which the Spirit of God and of truth may be 'recognized' (4:2,6) and claims made in the name of the Spirit can be tested. First, those who do in fact speak by the Spirit of truth will acknowledge rather than deny the truth about Jesus Christ (4:3 *cf* 2:18-20). Second, those who speak for God will first have listened to God. And the way to listen to God, according to John, is to listen to 'us', that is, to John and his associates who were the true witnesses of the Life which appeared in Jesus Christ (4:6 *cf* 1:1-4). Set in the midst of John's appeal we find an affirmation which is intended to motivate the believers. They are able to test the spirits and evaluate what they hear because of who they are and because of the victory which the indwelling Spirit of God gives them over the world, its viewpoint and it spokesmen (4:4-5).

In 1 John 4:7, the focus shifts from spiritual discernment back to the important theme of love for the brothers, love which is the necessary mark of believers because God Himself is love (4:8). 4:7 thus marks the beginning of a new section of the letter. Although this theme of brotherly love was in fact the subject of 3:11-24, it would be quite incorrect to view 4:1-6 as a digression. As we have already noted the passage with its call for discernment is an integral part of John's argument against the worldly influence of those who had broken away from the church and who were seeking to lead others astray.

Working through the text

As we have already noted above, the form of address 'dear friends' (*lit* beloved ones) with which John begins this paragraph is not new to his readers. Here, as elsewhere in the letter, it serves to remind the readers that they are indeed beloved, both by God the Father and by John and his associates. Such a reminder is of the utmost importance at this point in the letter for John wants his readers to understand that the appeal that follows does not arise out of self-interest but out of genuine love for them and in the name of the Father who loves them. There are many voices in the world each claiming to speak for God and each claiming to have the hearers' best interests at heart. John's readers must choose which voice they are going to heed and which viewpoint they are going to accept.

Strikingly enough, the appeal that John makes in 4:1 is not that the readers simply adopt John's point of view.

Rather, it is an appeal 'to test the spirits to see whether they are from God'. John's readers are thus called upon to exercise spiritual discernment and to evaluate everything they hear, John's words included, against the truth that they already know. Such discernment is of the utmost importance because 'many false prophets have gone out into the world'. The words 'gone out' are particularly striking and identify these 'false prophets' with the secessionists who 'went out' from among the believers (2:19) and thus with the many antichrists who have come (2:18) and are 'now already in the world' (4:3 NIV and KJV).

It is this identification of the false prophets with the antichrists that provides the readers with the first of two criteria by which they are to evaluate what they hear. The statement 'this is how you recognize the Spirit of God' (4:2) is equivalent to 'this is how you discern who truly speaks by the Spirit of God'. Those who truly speak for God and by His Spirit will acknowledge the truth that Jesus is indeed the Christ 'come in the flesh' (4:2). The word 'flesh' is used only here in relation to the person of Jesus, and is a strong one. It refers to the 'incarnation' of the Christ, the Divine Son, 'incarnation' not for its own sake, but as we have already noted with reference to 2:2 and will see again with reference to 4:10 and 5:6, incarnation with a view to atonement for sins.

The word translated 'acknowledge' is literally 'confess'. It is used in 1:9 for 'confession of sin' but its primary use in 1 John is with respect to confessing Jesus as the Christ. It is used in 2:23 to affirm that 'whoever confesses the Son has the Father also' – this in contrast to the liars and antichrists who deny that 'Jesus is the Christ' and who, by implication therefore have neither the Son nor the Father.

It is used in 4:15 to affirm that if anyone 'acknowledges that Jesus is the Son of God, God lives in them and they in God' (see below). And, as noted above, it is used in 4:2-3 to provide one of the two criteria by which the words of those who claim to speak in the name of the Spirit of God may be judged. As in 2:23 and 4:15 the criterion is the same. The one who truly speaks by the Spirit will confess that 'Jesus Christ has come in the flesh' (4:2), that is, that God's Christ, the Divine Son, and the Jesus of history are indeed one and the same Person. By contrast, those who 'do not confess Jesus' (i.e. who deny that Jesus is the Christ come in the flesh) (4:3; *cf* 2:22) do not speak by the Spirit of God or for God. Here, as elsewhere in 1 John, to be anti-Jesus is to be anti-Christ and thus not to be 'from God'!

In 4:4, the form of address changes from 'dear friends' to 'dear children'. Although this form of address does include John's relationship with his readers and serves to reinforce his love and concern for them, it is particularly the readers' status as 'children of God' that John has in mind. This is made clear in the following description 'you...are from God'. Furthermore, those who are from God have already overcome 'them', that is, the false prophets and the antichrists. John's use of the perfect tense 'have overcome' is important and points back to an event in the past which is the basis of the readers' present and future victory over their opponents. The question, of course, is: What event is John referring to? Comparison with 2:12-14 where the phrase 'have overcome' is used for the first time suggests that the overcoming took place at the moment when the readers' sins were forgiven on account of Jesus' name, that is, at the point of their conversion. This view is supported by 4:4 where their victory is said to be because of the one who is within them, surely a reference back to the Holy Spirit (3:24), the anointing that each believer received at the beginning when the truth was heard and believed (*cf* 2:24-27).

Although the believers are said to have overcome, John attributes the ultimate source of their victory to the greatness of the one who is within them. In their own strength, the believers are no match for the deceptive teaching of the false prophets because the latter are inspired and empowered by the one who is in the world (4:4), the 'evil one' who is the master of falsehood . His presence in the world deceives the world with the result that the 'viewpoint of the world' (4:5) stands in direct opposition to the viewpoint that comes from God (4:6). This is particularly true with reference to the truth about Jesus. The evil one stands against the truth that Jesus is the Christ and those who speak from his perspective will thus speak against Jesus. The fact that their 'ministry' is popular and the 'world listens to them' (4:5) should not unsettle the believers for the one who is in them is the 'Spirit of truth' (4:6) and the witness of the Spirit will always be to acknowledge that Jesus is the Christ (4:2; *cf* 2:20-23). Furthermore, since Jesus has overcome the evil one by His atoning death (2:2; 3:8), continued belief in this Jesus by the power of indwelling Spirit will give ongoing victory over the evil one and over those who speak for him in the world.

The statement that the world listens to the false prophets (4:5) prompts John to list the second criterion by which the 'spirits' may be tested. And it is a striking one, for it has to do not with speaking but listening! Those who belong to the truth and who speak the truth, says John, will listen to 'us' (4:6). While it is possible to take the 'us' as inclusive of

John and his readers (the 'you' of v. 4), it is surely preferable to see 'us' as a reference to John and his associates. This is particularly clear when we note the connection between the two criteria that John gives. The first criterion by which teaching is to be tested is that it confesses Jesus as the Christ come in the flesh. But since the coming of the Christ was an historical event it follows that such a confession of Christ must be based on eye-witness testimony to his coming. And as 1:1-4 makes clear, such testimony is unique to John and his associates. As eyewitnesses to the truth about Jesus the Christ, they spoke for God and from God and in the power of the anointing which comes from God, the Spirit of truth (4:4). But this would surely mean that anyone who refused to listen to the apostles would by definition be refusing to listen to the testimony of the Spirit of God. No matter how impressive and persuasive such a person's words may be, they were (and are) by definition false and should themselves be rejected by those wanting to know and continue in the truth. Thus the mark of the true preacher is that he will first listen to, then believe and finally proclaim as the truth the apostolic gospel about Jesus the Christ.

From text to message

One can hardly overstate the relevance or importance of this passage, especially at a time when the winds of false teaching blow across the church and many professing Christians seem to have lost their discernment. Much is claimed in the name of God and of the Spirit but far too little is said about Jesus and even less about the centrality of his atoning death. Whether it is the 'gospel minus' message of liberalism or the 'gospel plus' message of triumphalism, false prophets still trouble the church, proclaiming a cross-less Christianity that is a far cry from the gospel of Jesus and the apostles. Today, as in John's day, it is imperative for each believer to 'test the spirits' and to do so, not on the basis of personal subjective opinion or belief, no matter how sincere, but on the basis of the plain teaching of the Scriptures. Today, as in John's day, it is essential for us both to believe in and to proclaim Jesus Christ having come in the flesh, not merely to lift humanity to a higher life through an example of love, but to make atonement for the sins of the world.

It is worth noting the emphasis on the 'world' in 4:1-6. The word is used five times in six verses and reminds us that at its heart all false teaching is essentially worldly. This is what makes false teaching so dangerous and the need for discernment so urgent. The words of false teachers are words spoken from the viewpoint of the world, words that people's itching ears are longing to hear. The words of the gospel are words spoken from God's point of view and will only be heard and accepted through the work of the Spirit. The encouragement for preacher and hearer alike is, however, that the Spirit of God is greater than the spirit that is in the world and that by His grace and powerful work God's truth will prevail.

Getting the message clear: the theme

- Because there are many false teachers in the world who speak from the viewpoint of the world it is essential that every believer should test what is said before accepting it as true.

- The measure by which all teaching must be tested is the apostolic gospel about Jesus Christ. If any teaching, no matter how plausible it sounds, denies or downplays the centrality of Jesus, His mission and in particular His atoning death, such teaching should be rejected as false.

- Believers in Jesus the Christ can be confident and stand firm against false teaching because the Spirit of God within them will continue to testify to the truth about Jesus and enable them to keep on believing that truth.

Getting the message clear: the aim

To encourage believers to test what they hear against the apostolic gospel and to continue to stand firm in their faith in Jesus the Christ even in the face of the most plausible of arguments to the contrary.

A way in

One way in is to highlight how plausible and seductive false teaching can be. It seldom comes to us in clearly heretical terms, but rather in subtle variations of the truth, simply moving to the side what the gospel considers to be central. This is particularly true when it comes to teaching about Jesus. Jesus may well be praised, but the focus will have shifted away from the centrality of his death. Christmas cheer or moral example rather than Easter faith will be the hallmark of all nominal Christianity.

Another way in is to point out the danger that we all face when it comes to personal affirmation and acceptance. No one likes to be ridiculed or rejected. The danger of all false teaching is that it appeals to our desire to fit in rather than to stand out as odd. And this is particularly true when it comes to belief in Jesus. By and large, people will be positive about Jesus but negative about the so-called antiquated views about his deity, his death and resurrection. The world can live with respect for Jesus the good man, but personal faith in Jesus the dying, rising saviour of the world sets believers apart and such distinctiveness can be very uncomfortable for those who want to fit in. Peer pressure is a great enemy of Christian commitment.

Ideas for application

- Spiritual discernment is a vital but sadly rare virtue. The call to test the spirits underlines the importance of the right of private judgement among believers. Such discernment should be cultivated within the church today.

- If true discernment is to flourish, a culture of Biblical literacy and critical thinking needs to be encouraged within the local church. Whereas the true believer should never be sceptical of the teaching of the Scripture, it is always good to be sceptical of received opinions and interpretations of Scripture. Scripture alone must remain the rule of faith and conduct.

- Because the Person and Work of Christ are central to the teaching of authentic Christianity, false teaching will inevitably involve a false Christology. The key question to ask of any new teaching is 'What does it say about the Person and work of Christ?'

- Although false teachers use the Bible to establish their doctrine, they will invariably use the Bible in a way which does not respect the final authority of the apostolic gospel. 'Scripture plus' or 'scripture minus' has always been the feature of false teaching.

Suggestions for preaching

Sermon

Spiritual Discernment (1 John 4:1-6)

1. Introduction
    - The voice of the world – designer Christianity
    - The pull of the world – Christianity without cost
2. The Call for Discernment
    - Test the spirits because…
        - False prophets in the world
        - The world in the church
    - This is how you know
        - Gospel Truth (vv. 2-3)
        - Apostolic Authority (vv. 6)
3. An Encouragement for the Discerning
    - The One to whom you belong
    - The One who is within you

Suggestions for teaching

Questions to help understand the passage

1. In what different ways does John use the word 'spirit' in this passage?

2. Why are believers to 'test the spirits'?
3. What characterises the message of the false prophets?
4. Who does John have in mind with the pronouns 'you', 'they' and 'us'?
5. By what two criteria are the believers to test what they hear?
6. How does the message of the false prophets align with the viewpoint of the world? Why?
7. Who, according to this passage, are the ones who are 'from God'?
8. What fundamental contrasts does John draw in this passage?

Questions to help apply the passage

1. Why is discernment important today?
2. What is the current viewpoint of the world with respect to the Person and work of Christ?
3. What is the current viewpoint of the world with regard to the Apostolic Gospel and the New Testament Scriptures?
4. In what ways are Christians tempted to compromise with the viewpoint of the world?
5. In what way does this passage encourage discernment?
6. In what way does this passage encourage conviction and perseverance in the faith?

9
Knowing the Unseen God (1 John 4:7-21)

Introduction

In 1 John 3:23-24, John reminded his readers of God's command to persevere in faith and in love and of God's provision for them in the gift of His indwelling Spirit, by whom such perseverance in faith and love could be maintained. As we have seen, the background to this reminder was the bold and unsettling claims made by the secessionists, claims which John urged his readers both to test against the truth which they already knew and to withstand in the power of the Spirit (4:1-6). At the heart of these claims lay an essentially worldly point of view with respect to the nature of true relationship with God, a point of view which rejected the idea that God could only be known through Jesus Christ whom God had sent into the world to be its saviour (4:14). For the secessionists, the fact that God is Spirit and therefore unseen (note John's comments in 4:12 and 4:20) meant that God could only be known individually, spiritually and immediately. In such a view there was no place for Jesus the man as mediator between God and man. For John, the fact that God is unseen means that we can only know God if He intervenes in history and, in love, makes Himself known. And this is precisely what God did when He 'sent His Son Jesus as an atoning sacrifice for our sins' (4:10) in order that 'we might live through Him' (4:9 NIV and KJV).

John's point in 4:7-21 is crystal clear and deeply encouraging for all true believers. The God who is light and who has made his light shine in the world (1:5; 2:8) is the God who is love (4:8,16) and who, in Christ, has made His love known among us (4:9,10). And since this is so, it follows that those who truly know and love this unseen God will, by the power of His Spirit within them, continue to acknowledge Jesus as the Christ, the Son of God and to love those who like them are believers in Jesus. It is within this community of faith and love that the Spirit of God is at work and the true knowledge of God is found.

Listening to the text

Context and structure

In 1 John 4:7-21, there is a change of tone and theme from the previous paragraph. As in 4:1, the direct form of address 'dear friends' marks the beginning of a new section and provides the basis for the appeal which follows. The negative imperative of 4:1: 'do not believe every spirit, but test the spirits' gives way to the positive exhortation of 4:7: 'let us love one another' (NIV and KJV). Thus the claims of the secessionists, so much the focus of 4:1-6 (as they were of 2:18-27), are shifted to the background, although, as we saw above, they are not entirely lost from view. In focus once again are the four distinguishing hallmarks of the true Christian, namely, love for the children of God (4:7-12,19-21), faith in Jesus as the Christ (4:13-16), obedience to God's word expressed in Christlikeness (4:17) and the witness of the indwelling Spirit (4:13). Such a shift of focus shows that John's primary aim in the passage was to strengthen the assurance of those who belong to the truth. John's aim in this passage is thus completely in line with his purpose in writing the letter as a whole (see 5:13).

The passage begins and ends with a reference to the love that true believers are to have for one another (4:7,21). Indeed, the reference to God's command in 4:21 takes the reader back to the summary statement in 3:23-24 where the same four hallmarks of the true Christian are listed. Of these four, love is certainly the one which is emphasised in 4:7-21 as it was in 3:11-24, but, as we saw above, not to the absolute exclusion of the others. This emphasis on love is entirely understandable given John's two-fold declaration that God is love (4:8,16), a declaration that controls the main argument of the passage as a whole. The passage can be sub-divided into four closely connected parts, namely 4:7-12, 4:13-16a, 4:16b-18 and 4:19-21. In each part the love of God is emphasised and each is designed to assure the readers of the reality of their relationship with the God who loves them.

Before leaving this section, a comment must be made in defence of the decision to end with 4:21 rather than with 5:4 or 5:5 as many of the commentaries do. Certainly the theme of faith in Jesus as the Son of God with which 5:1 begins is present in 4:15 and the themes of love and obedience, found in 4:7-21 are clearly echoed in 5:2-5. Furthermore, 5:1 also echoes the teaching of 4:7 that the true believer has been born of God as well as the use of the term 'everyone' (*lit.* 'all who'; see 5:1 and 4:7; *cf* 2:29; 3:3-4;

5:4). Thus the argument for including at least part of 5:1-5 with 4:7-21 seems to be very strong, perhaps viewed as a summary statement as was the case with 3:23-24.

In my opinion, however, the similarity of 5:1-5 to the summary statement in 3:23-24 plus the re-introduction of the words 'world' and 'overcome' in 5:4-5 (*cf* 2:15-17; 4:4-6), suggest that 5:1-5 is to be taken as a section in its own terms, summarising previous arguments and bringing the second part of the letter to a conclusion. This would, of course, mean that 5:6-12 be taken as a section on its own.

Working through the text

Knowing the God who is love (4:7-12)

The paragraph begins in customary fashion with an appeal to the 'dear friends', those who are 'beloved' both by John and by God (*see above*). As those who have experienced the love of God made known in Christ (*see below*), believers ought to 'love one another' (4:7), that is 'continue to love one another', as they had done from the beginning of their inclusion into the community of believers in Jesus (*cf* 3:11). This appeal to continue in brotherly love is then followed by two reasons why love for one another is a necessary characteristic of every true believer.

First, John reminds his readers that God is the source of love and since 'love comes from God' it follows that 'everyone who loves has been born of God and knows God' (4:7). It is important to note John's use of the perfect tense 'has been born of God' for John is presenting brotherly love as evidence of regeneration rather than the basis of a relationship with God. Furthermore the additional descriptor 'and knows God' is a reminder that it is those who have been born of God who are in fellowship with God. This is, of course, precisely what the secessionists would have claimed for themselves but with two notable differences. First, their claim to knowledge of God was exclusive, reserved only for those who followed their teaching. To this, John's response is to declare that *everyone* who loves their fellow believers has been born of God and knows God. Second, their claim to knowledge of God had little or no practical effect, especially when it came to relationships with fellow believers. Thus in countering their exclusivity, John applies his own exclusion, namely that *whoever* does not live in love does in fact not know God, whatever claims they may make. Behind this statement we find the second of the two reasons that John gives for his claim that love for one another is a necessary characteristic of every true believer. Those who are born of God and know God will love one another because 'God is love' (4:8). It is because God is love that love comes from God and those who know God love one another.

In 4:9-10, John substantiates the claim that God is love. John's argument is important because the invisibility of God (4:12) could lead to ambiguity as far as evidence for the knowledge of God is concerned. Since 'no one has ever seen God' (4:12) how can anyone claim to truly know God or say with authority that God is love. The answer lies in the fact that the God who is love has in fact 'showed his love among us' (4:9). The word translated 'showed' is the word 'appeared', a word that John uses in particular to speak about the 'appearing of the Son of God' in history (see e.g. 1:2; 3:5,8) and again at the end of the age (3:2). In 4:9, the appearing of the love of God in the world is synonymous with the sending by God of His One and Only Son into the world. The love of the invisible God is thus made visible in and through His Son sent into the world!

Nor is this love of God in sending His Son merely for revelatory purposes. The coming of Christ which makes the love of God visible is also so that 'we might have life through Him' (4:9). In the context of 4:7 this 'life' through Christ is the eternal life which consists of knowing God through Jesus Christ whom He has sent (*cf* 1:2; 2:25; 5:11-12). But such life in relationship with God is only possible if sin has been atoned for since, as John stated right at the outset of his letter, God is light and no one who is in the darkness can have fellowship with Him (1:5-7). Fellowship with the God who is light is thus only possible because of the loving initiative of the God who is love, the God who in love sent His Son into the world 'as an atoning sacrifice for our sins' (4:10). True relationship with God thus begins not with our love for God, but with His love for us, love made manifest in Jesus Christ, the atoning sacrifice for our sins. Thus, as John has already stated and will state again (*see below*), it is only through this Jesus that God can truly be known.

The recognition that God has loved all believers in Christ in this way means that they must also love one another in the same way that God has loved them. For those who are God's beloved (4:11) the '*so*' (i.e. manner not extent) of God's love in Christ creates both an example of love (*cf* 3:16) and an obligation to love. This is what John means when he writes 'since God so loved us, we also ought to love one another' (4:11). It is, thus, in love for one another that God's love in Christ is 'made complete', that is, accomplishes its goal.

Relying upon the God who is love (4:13-16)

In 4:13, John returns to a fuller expression of a statement made in 3:24. On both occasions he uses the language of assurance, namely, 'this is how we know'. The 'we' in these statements refers both to John and his readers, those within whom the Lord 'lives' or *lit* 'remains'. The focus is both upon what is known – 'he lives in us' (3:24) or 'we live in Him and He is us' (4:13) – and upon how we know, namely, 'because He has given us His Spirit' (4:13; *cf* 3:24). In 3:24, this gift of the Spirit as the basis of knowing was left to stand largely unqualified, although the statement did lead directly to a discussion about the importance of discernment and the centrality of a true confession of Jesus as the Christ as the necessary mark of every true believer in whom God lived by His Spirit (see 4:1-6). In 4:13, this fact of the indwelling Spirit is again linked to the confession of Jesus as the Christ, the Son of God (4:15), a confession made on the basis of the testimony of the eyewitness to the Father's sending of His Son. John and his associates have 'seen and testify that the Father has sent His Son to be the saviour of the world' (4:14). This testimony is reliable and trustworthy and should thus be received by all as the basis of a true relationship with God. And the way to receive this testimony and enter into fellowship with the God who sent his Son is by 'acknowledging' (*lit* confessing) 'that Jesus is the Son of God' (4:15). Those who acknowledge Jesus in this way are themselves saved and enter into a true and living relationship with God. It is they and they alone who know and can rely upon the love of God (4:16).

Confidence before the God who is love (4:16b-18)

The 'love that God has for us' and upon which all who acknowledge Jesus as the Son of God and the Saviour of the world can 'rely' arises, of course, from the fact that God Himself is love. John thus restates this key theological declaration (4:16b) and again connects it to the life of love that must characterise everyone in whom this God lives. Alongside faith in Jesus as the Christ – faith made possible through the inner work of the Spirit – love for one another must be in evidence in the true believer. It is not just that love for others and faith in Jesus are complementary, it is that love and faith are necessarily linked – both must be present. This is John's point in 4:17. Those who 'live in love' (4:16b) demonstrate that God's love in Christ has been brought to its desired goal, namely love for other believers. But this life of love is in fact a life modelled upon the life of Jesus Himself, for He is the concrete expression of the love of God. Thus those who have come to acknowledge Jesus as God's Son their Saviour will by the work of God's Spirit within them also begin to imitate His (that is *Jesus'*) way of life (4:17). And that way of life is the way of love, lived out in practice, 'in this world' (4:17).

This is what John means when he speaks about 'perfect love' (4:18). He is not referring to the love that God has for us in Christ, perfect though that is. John is referring to God's love perfected, that is, 'made complete' in us, namely true love arising out of faith in Christ. It is this love which 'drives out fear' (4:18), giving the believer 'confidence on the day of judgement' (4:17). Such confidence before the Lord is a far cry from the presumptuous claims of the secessionists for it is not based upon personal merit, but upon God's work for us in the death of Jesus and then in us by the work of His Spirit. It is this same confidence that John had in mind when he assured his readers that by remaining in Jesus the Christ, they could be 'confident and unashamed before Him at His coming' (2:28). The opposite of this confidence is fear, fear arising from the fact that the one fearing has not grasped the reality of God's love in Christ and the full atonement for sins provided in the death of Jesus. Sin unatoned for will, indeed, lead to punishment on the Day of Judgement and those whose sins have not been forgiven do well to fear that day. But such fear is entirely out of place for those who have received God's love and who have come to confess Jesus as the Christ. Faith in Christ expressing itself in love for one another is the mark of the true child of God and no child need fear in the presence of a loving Father.

Obeying the God who is love (4:19-21)

The truth that God is indeed the loving Father who in love sent His Son into the world to save sinners (4:14) lays the foundation for John to refer to his readers as members of this family of love. The God who is love (4:8,16) has taken the initiative to love. In John's words 'God first loved us' and it is for this reason that 'we do love' (4:19) and indeed 'must love' (4:21). Once again the claims and the actions of the secessionists are in view. 'Whoever claims to love God and yet hates a brother or sister is a liar' (4:20). And the reason behind such a statement is now of course crystal clear. The love of the unseen God (4:12) has been seen in the love of Jesus Christ who came into the world to save sinners. God's love in Christ is thus undeserved but also incarnational and sacrificial, as John stated it earlier, 'not love with words or speech' alone but love 'in action and in truth' (3:18). And since God's love was undeserved, incarnational and also sacrificial, such love must be evident among those who claim to know this God. Failure to love those whom God has loved is thus not to be of God or of the truth, but to be a liar. Failure to love others in the community, no matter how undeserving they may be, is to show that one has not understood or indeed experienced the love of God. God's incarnational love in Christ must and will be expressed 'incarnationally' i.e. within the community and in practice not abstractedly or merely in word alone.

And thus we are brought full circle to the point at which our paragraph as a whole began. In 4:7, John urged his readers to 'love one another because love comes from God'. In 4:21 he reminds them that this God who is love and who has loved us in Christ has given us this command: 'Anyone who loves God must also love their brother and sister.'

From text to message

John's two-fold declaration that God is love (4:8,16) is probably the best known and, at one level at least, the most widely accepted New Testament statement about God. Many who reject the idea of God as holy or righteous or good would affirm that God, if He exists at all, must indeed be a loving God. And so it is tempting for the preacher, presented with these statements about God, to use 1 John 4:7-21 as a platform to talk about the fact of God's love, the way in which this love of God has been manifested in our fallen and broken world and the implications of this love of God for all who experience it. And, as we have noted above, John certainly does speak about the fact and nature and implications of the love of God in this passage.

And yet, as we have also noted, John has placed this teaching about the God who is love within a very particular context and applied it for a very particular purpose. For this teaching about the God who is love is directed not to the curious outsider but to the troubled and unsettled insider and is designed to establish those who have experienced

God's love in that love. Thus while the passage begins with an exhortation to love (4:7) and ends with a reminder of God's command to love (4:21), it is, at its heart, a way of knowing that we know the God who is love (4:7,8) and a basis for relying in full confidence upon this God (4:16,17).

Given the length of the passage it is probably best to deal with it in a series of talks based upon the divisions as set out in the discussion of the text as above.

Getting the message clear: the theme

For the passage as a whole:-

The God who is love has made His love known by sending His Son as an atoning sacrifice for sin. This act of love at God's initiative gives us confidence before Him, both now and on the Day of Judgement. Is also necessitates our response of daily love for fellow believers.

For the individual paragraphs:

- Though God is unseen, He has revealed Himself in the death of Christ as the God who is love. This act of God's love in Christ is entirely at God's initiative and obligates true believers to take the initiative in loving one another.
- Because God's love has been made manifest in His Son, those who have experienced the love of God will of necessity recognise and confess faith in Jesus Christ, the Son of God.
- Those who have experienced God's love in Christ and who trust in Christ will be able to stand before God with confidence on the Day of Judgement and live with assurance before God in this life.

- Those who have experienced God's love will of necessity love one another.

Getting the message clear: the aim

- To assure those who have put their trust in Christ that they do indeed know the God who is love and to encourage them to keep on relying upon the God who has loved them in Christ.
- To exhort those who have experienced God's love in Christ to keep on loving one another.

A way in

A way in to talk 1 could be to highlight the challenge posed by the invisibility of God. Since we cannot see God, how can we know what He is like or if He loves us? Circumstances are ambiguous and the statement 'God loves you' often seems to fall flat in the face of difficult times. Added to this is the question, how can we express our love for the invisible intangible God. 1 John 4:7-12 takes our difficulty seriously and reminds us that the love of the invisible God has in fact been made visible in Christ. And our love for the invisible God will be made visible in our love for one another.

A way into talk 2 could be to speak about the relationship between subjective experience and objective evidence. There is a subjective side to our Christian faith – what John refers to as our 'knowing'. But our knowing is not independent of God's 'making known' which He has done in particular in Christ. Our truly knowing God who is love is thus closely tied to our confessing the Lord Jesus who makes God known as saviour of the world. This leads us into talking about the fact that we can rely on God's love for us in Christ and thus know for certain that we know Him.

A way into talk 3 could be to speak about the reality of God's judgement of the world. Because God is love, He must and will hold people accountable for their conduct. Love and accountability go hand in hand. Since we are sinners, the thought of facing God on the Day of Judgement fills us with dread. But the true believer need not fear the thought of facing God. On the contrary, the love of God in Christ and at work in us gives us confidence to stand before God on that Day.

A way into talk 4 could be to talk about the relationship between love and obedience. Can we be commanded to love one another? If love were an emotion the answer is, of course, 'No'. But if love is in fact the way we act toward those around us – a visible demonstration of love – then we can be commanded to love. This is particularly true of God's love expressed in and through our love for one another.

Ideas for application

- The death of Jesus makes the love of the invisible God visible among us. For this reason love must be made visible within the Christian community. Invisible love is not love at all.
- The love of God in Jesus Christ comes to us not in response to our love but at God's initiative. Thus we should take the initiative in loving one another.
- Our love for God expressed in love for one another is one of the objectives that Christ sought to accomplish by His death. Love for one another thus shows that God's love in us has achieved its goal.
- Love for God, faith in Christ and love for one another are all necessary and inter-related

characteristics of those who know God and have experienced His love.

- The love of God shown in Christ enables us to rely on God's love for us and gives us assurance in our relationship with Him.
- Those who love one another in response to God's love for them in Christ truly know God and can have confidence before Him on the Day of Judgement. Knowing that we can stand before God with confidence on that Day is part of what it means to have assurance.
- Love is a way of life rather than a way of feeling. For this reason it can be commanded. Because we remain sinners even as believers, love must also be commanded.

Suggestions for preaching

Sermon 1

Knowing the God who is love (4:7-12)

1. Introduction
    - The problem of the Unseen God
    - Loved by the Unseen God
    - Love for the Unseen God
2. God's Love made visible
    - God is love
    - God's love made visible in Christ

    - God's initiative in love
    - Christ's atonement because of love

3. Responding to God's love
    - 'Let us love one another'
    - 'We ought to love one another'

Sermon 2

Relying on the God who is love (4:13-16a)

1. Introduction
    - How we know that we know…
2. The Spirit and the Word
    - God has given us His Spirit
    - God has sent His Son
    - The Apostolic testimony
    - Confessing the Son in the power of the Spirit
3. Knowing God's love in Jesus
    - The Spirit enables us to acknowledge God's love in Christ
4. Relying on God's love in Jesus
    - The Spirit enables us to rely on God's love in Christ

Sermon 3

Confidence before the God of love (4:16b-18)

1. Introduction
    - The God of love and the Day of Judgement

2. Living in Love
    - God is love
    - God's love made complete
    - Christ-like love in this world
3. Fear expelled by love
    - Fear and judgement
    - Love and confidence
4. Confident in God's love made complete

Sermon 4

Obeying the God who is love (4:19-21)

1. Introduction
    - Commanded to love?
2. We love because...
    - God's loving initiative
    - Whoever claims to love...
    - Whoever does not love...
    - Love among the loved
3. The command to love
    - A logical response
    - A necessary response

Suggestions for teaching

Questions to help understand the passage

1. Why does John address his readers as 'dear friends' (*beloved*) at the start of this passage?

2. According to this passage, where does love come from?

3. What characterises this love that comes from God?

4. How is love defined in this passage?

5. What is true of those who will not live in love? Why?

6. In what way does this passage deal with the challenge that arises from the fact that God is unseen?

7. How can believers know that they 'live in God' according to this passage?

8. What lies at the heart of the apostolic testimony about the Father and the Son?

9. What is the right response to this testimony?

10. In what way does the love of God brought to completion relate to confidence on the Day of Judgement?

11. In what way are fear and love mutually exclusive?

12. Throughout the passage John stresses that God takes the initiative in showing His love. In what way is this fact important to John's argument?

13. How are love and obedience related?

Questions to help apply the passage

1. What reasons does John give to motivate believers to love one another?

2. How are love for the brothers and personal assurance connected?

3. What are the practical implications of the fact that God is love?

4. Words like 'rely' and 'confidence' are words of great importance in our present world where so many are filled with doubt and insecurity. How does this passage enable us to lay a foundation for true spiritual confidence?

5. In what way does God's initiative taking love in Christ challenge our thinking about who we should love and how we should express such love?

6. According to this passage, how would you define 'The Complete Christian'?

7. How does this passage enable us to evaluate the validity of claims to know God?

8. In what way does this passage undermine Christian elitism?

10

The Victorious Life (1 John 5:1-5)

Introduction

In 1 John 3:23, John reminded his readers of God's two-fold command, namely, 'to believe in the name of His Son, Jesus Christ, and to love one another as He commanded us'. As we saw in our discussion of that passage, this brief statement brings together three key identifying marks of those who truly know God, namely, obedience to God, faith in Jesus and love for the brothers. We also saw that these characteristics of the true Christian were mentioned precisely because of the lingering influence of a group of teachers who were once part of the community, but had left it because they had departed from the apostolic gospel about Jesus the Christ. John's main aim was thus to assure those who remained that they were in fact truly born of God and thus in true fellowship with Him. Having warned explicitly against these false prophets in 4:1-6, John turned to the second of the two commands, namely love for the brothers in 4:7-21, urging his readers to live a life of love for one another because God is love and because God had in love reached out to them in the death of Jesus.

In 5:1-5, the focus is upon the first of God's commands given in 3:23, namely, the command to believe in Jesus Christ His Son. The passage begins and ends with a reference to active faith and stresses the now familiar idea that such faith must have a specific content and focus. True faith is belief that 'Jesus is the Christ...the Son of God' (5:1,5). Nor is such faith optional for those who claim to have been born of God, for John stresses both the inclusivity and the exclusivity of faith. *Everyone* who believes has been born of God, which of course implies that *everyone* who is born of God must believe and *anyone* who does not believe in Jesus has not been born of God. Indeed, as we shall see below, it is this faith alone which is the key to a life of victory over the world (5:4). Important though faith is, it never stands alone in the Christian life and so, in keeping with the theme of the letter as a whole, we also find references to obedience to God's commands and love for fellow believers as the measure of authenticity alongside of authentic faith in Christ. Together these are true evidences of spiritual regeneration.

Listening to the text

Context and structure

The references to love for God's children in 5:1-2 and the absence of any reference to the love imperative after 5:3b have led many commentators to see 5:1-4a as part of the previous passage rather than to see 5:1-5 as a section in its own right. In this view the statement 'for everyone born of God overcomes the world' (5:4a) ends the section begun in 4:7 and introduces the next section, 5:4b-12, which has its focus on faith arising out of the testimony about the Son of God. There is much to be said for this view, especially since the reference to acknowledging that Jesus is the Son of God (4:15) ties in closely with the references to faith in 5:1 and the references to love in 5:1-2 do seem to be an extension of the discussion begun in 4:7. Furthermore, there is nothing textual to prevent a new section beginning with 'this is the victory…' (5:4b), although the word 'and' in the original suggests that 5:4a and 5:4b are more closely connected than it appears in translation. Others, perhaps in the light of this point, but still seeing the link with 4:7ff, have extended the section to include 5:5 as well with the result that the new section consists of 5:6-12 (see explanation below).

On balance, however, it seems preferable to treat 5:1-5 as a section in its own right. First, as noted above, it does seem to be an elaboration of the command to believe in Jesus in 3:23, in parallel with rather than as part of the command to love one another which was the focus of 4:7-21. Second, although the word 'world' is used in 4:9 and 4:14, its use there is with reference to the mission of Jesus to save the world rather than with the idea of 'overcoming the world' as in 5:4-5. This reference to overcoming the world links 5:1-5 more closely with 2:15-17 and 4:1-6 than with 4:7-21. Third, the statement 'This is the one who came…' in 5:6 as an elaboration of what it means for Jesus to be the Christ, the Son of God suggests that if anything 5:1-5 belongs with the passage that follows rather than the one that precedes. Given the arguments that can be offered on both sides, it is, perhaps, best to identify 1 John 5:1-5 as one of the bridge sections that are so typical of the letter and to focus on its rich content rather than its particular place in the structure of the letter. Given this approach to 5:1-5, we will treat the following section, namely 5:6-12, as a closely related but self-contained section which brings that main body of the letter to a conclusion.

Working through the text

As we noted above, the term 'everyone' with which John begins this section is both inclusive and exclusive. Over and against the secessionists who claimed special knowledge or fellowship with God, John affirms that every true believer has indeed been born of God. No one who is part of God's family by virtue of their faith in Christ should be viewed or treated as an outsider. At the same time, however, there is a very real exclusivity, one which God Himself has established and which hinges on saving faith in Christ. The *everyone* of 5:1 implies a *no one*. Since everyone who believes that Jesus is the Christ has been born of God then, by implication, no one who denies that Jesus is the Christ has been born of God (*cf* 2:22-23; 4:3). This is precisely the point that John makes at the end of the section where he states 'only the one who believes that Jesus is the Son of God' overcomes the world (5:5).

Three additional points are worth noting. First, it is important to note that John is not speaking about faith in Christ as something static, a mere fact of belief. His use of the present participle 'the one believing' (5:1,5) can be translated 'believes and continues to believe'. John is thus both assuring his readers who, unlike the secessionists, do hold a living faith in Christ that they are the true children of God and urging them to persevere in this faith. That is of course precisely what the secessionists had failed to do. Second, John's use of the perfect tense 'has been born' of God is important and reminds the readers that the act of believing arises out of the new birth rather than being the cause of it. It is for this reason that faith in Christ can be used as evidence of having been born of God. Third, the statement 'Jesus is the Christ' which is the content of what the 'believing' must be at this point in the letter includes all that John has said thus far about what it means for Jesus to be the Christ. We will return to this point again in reference to 5:6, but is worth noting here. For Jesus to be the Christ, the Son of God (5:1,5), is for Jesus to be the one who was with the Father and who appeared in visible, tangible flesh (1:1,2; 4:2), the Righteous One who made atonement for the sins of the world (2:1,2; 4:10), the one sent by the Father who came to take away sin, to destroy the devil's work and in so doing to be the saviour of the world (see 3:5-8; 4:9-14). It is ongoing faith in this Jesus that brings life and it is this faith alone which identifies the true children of God.

Having re-stated the importance of faith in Christ as an identifying mark of every new born child of God, John returns to the theme of love for the brothers. Those who have been born of God (5:1) will of necessity love the One, who through this gift of new birth, has become their Father. But it surely follows that those who truly love God their Father will also love the one who has been born of God. Some take this to be a reference to Jesus, the Son of God, interpreting the words 'having been born of him' in the original to refer to the eternal begetting of the Son by the Father. In this view John's point is that those who have been born of God believe that Jesus is the Christ and have love for Jesus, the One born of God. Taken in context, however, it is surely better to interpret the phrase 'the one born of God' to refer to others who likewise have been born of God and thus believe that Jesus is the Christ. First, it is worth noting that though faith in Jesus is often mentioned as a hallmark of the true child of God, the fact or necessity of love for Jesus is not mentioned anywhere else in the letter. John's use of recapitulation makes a single reference highly unlikely. Second, the immediate context suggests that the phrase 'the one born of him' should be understood to refer to fellow believers in Jesus. In 5:2 the statement 'this is how we know that we love the children of God' does not begin a new idea but continues the idea begun in the previous sentence. The antecedent of the words 'children of God' in 5:2 is 'the one born of God' in 5:1 with the result that the two are synonymous. John's point in 5:1b is thus that those who are born of God and who believe that Jesus is the Christ will love others who have been born of God and who likewise believe that Jesus is the Christ. Indeed, as he stated in 4:20, love for the children of God is one visible expression of love for God and thus a measure of the truth of one's claim to love God.

It is this close connection between love for God and love for the children of God which leads to the rather surprising statement in 5:2. We might have expected 'this is how we know that we love God: by loving the children of God', but in fact John reverses the order. Literally John says: 'This is how we know that we love the children of God: when we love God and when we keep his commands'. Indeed, John goes on to state that 'to keep God's commands...is love for God' (5:3).

According to John then, whereas love for the children of God and obedience to God's commands are the true and necessary expressions of what it means in practice to love God, love for God is absolutely essential if one is to love God's children and keep His commands. Furthermore, given the connection of both love for the brothers and obedience to

God's commands to the love of God, it follows that both love and obedience must characterise those who love God. Surprising though John's wording is, his main point is thus crystal clear and is made in a way that highlights the stark contrast between those who hold firm to John's teaching and the secessionists. The secessionists claim to know and love God, but they neither love the brothers nor do they obey God's commands. Thus their claim to love God is proved false. John's readers, having stayed true to what was taught in the beginning, love fellow believers and seek to do God's commands. In this they show that it is they and not the secessionists who truly love God.

The fact that love for God is seen in obedience to His commands, leads John to a further point of contrast between those who have been born of God and those who have not. Those who have been born of God and who love God do not find His commands 'burdensome' (5:3). Prior to this act of divine regeneration it was characteristic of people to 'love the world and the things of the world' (2:15) and to 'walk in the darkness' (1:6). Having been born of God, however, love for the world is replaced by love for God and for fellow believers and a new desire is born to walk in the light and to enjoy fellowship first with God and then with those who belong to the light (1:5-7). Those who have been born of God can thus be said to have 'overcome the world' because of the work of God within them (5:4).

But where does this work of God within His children begin? From the point of view of divine initiative, it begins with God for they *have been* born of God. But from the point of view of human experience it begins with their faith in Jesus Christ as the Son of God (5:4b,5). As John has already made clear, in order to overcome the world one also needs to overcome the evil one and the starting point for this victory is to have one's sins forgiven in the name of Jesus who made an atonement for sin (2:12-13; *cf* 2:2). It is through Jesus alone that the work of the devil is destroyed (3:8) and through Jesus alone that salvation therefore comes into the world to save those who are held in bondage by the world (*cf* 4:7-16). Apart from the atonement of the incarnate Christ, there can be neither salvation nor victory over the world or the evil one who holds the world in his grip. But since the Christ has come in the flesh in the person of Jesus and atonement has been made by Him, the one who believes that Jesus is the Son of God (5:5) and who entrusts himself or herself to His saving work has indeed overcome the world and is saved.

From text to message

Despite its brevity, 1 John 5:1-5 highlights two important and relevant truths, truths that need to be reinforced in our day. The first of these truths concerns what we described above as the inclusivity and the exclusivity of the truth about Jesus. We live in an age when talk of exclusivity is considered to be in bad taste if not in contradiction of our fundamental rights as people. And this is especially true when it comes to talk about God. When it comes to God, everyone is in irrespective of what they believe and no one is to be considered as excluded.

John's teaching, however, stands in stark contrast to the popular view. While he is quite willing to use words like 'everyone' to counter a wrong spiritual elitism and exclusivity, John is also quite willing to use words like 'no one' and 'only' to destroy a false presumption. And the key to John's view on these matters is the person of Jesus. Thus unlike many today John is quick to emphasise the uniqueness of Jesus and the absolute necessity of faith in Jesus, not as we imagine Him to be but as He is made known to us in the apostolic gospel. And as we shall see again in the next passage, John's repeated emphasis on the need for faith in Jesus is not only to assure those who do believe but also to warn and protect those who are in danger of giving way to the spirit of the age.

The second important and relevant truth highlighted in 1 John 5:1-5 is the truth that the normal Christian life is meant to be a life of victory rather than of defeat. Such language can, of course, be misleading if not properly understood, but it is the language that John uses and for good reason. In our passage, as in the rest of the letter, John insists that a credible profession of faith should always be accompanied by true evidence of faith. Faith in Jesus is indeed life transforming and will, as we have already seen, manifest itself in love for others and obedience to God. The fact that John repeats these practical evidences of faith as often as he does throughout the letter and, in particular, in summary passages such as 5:1-5 must surely remind us of their importance for the church today.

Getting the message clear: the theme

Every true believer in Jesus the Christ, the Son of God, has been born of God and has by faith overcome the world. This victorious life is characterised by love for God shown in practical love for fellow believers and a joyful commitment to obeying God's commands.

Getting the message clear: the aim

- To assure those who believe that Jesus is the Christ, the Son of God that it is they who have truly been born of God and who thus have victory over the world.

- To remind those who claim to have been born of God and to love God that faith in Jesus, love for fellow believers and obedience to God's commands are all inseparable evidences of the true knowledge of God.

A way in

One way in could be to begin by speaking about the possibility of the 'Victorious Christian Life'. Although the phrase has been abused and could sound triumphalistic, it nevertheless captures the idea, fundamental to John's teaching, that the believer in Jesus does and should have victory over the world and over the evil one and that this victory should be seen in the daily life of every believer. Indeed, one could argue that one reason why wrong understandings of the 'Victorious Christian Life' abound is that the evangelical church is so often silent on the subject. In his first letter, John is certainly a keen advocate of a life of victory for the believer. But, as we shall see in 1 John 5:1-5, the twist in the tail of John's teaching is that the 'Victorious Christian Life' is, in practice, nothing more but certainly nothing less than the normal Christian life of persevering faith in Jesus, wholehearted love for fellow believers and joyful obedience to God's commands.

Another way in would be to raise the questions about exclusivity and inclusivity with respect to relationship with God. As we noted above, people today view claims for the uniqueness of Christ and the necessity of faith in Jesus in a very hostile light. And yet we may well ask the question whether such a content-less, generalised faith is in fact meaningful in any real way. If faith is not to fall into the trap of being a mere fanaticism (an exceedingly dangerous thing!) then surely faith must have a focus and a clear content. In 1 John 5:1 and 5 in particular, we are reminded of what such a focus and content must be if our faith is to be distinctively Christian. But we are also reminded that such faith if it is to be real does not stand alone but is in fact life-changing. Faith and good deeds are thus not enemies but close allies in authentic Christianity.

Ideas for application

- Note that John's *everyone* in 5:1 and 5 also implies a *no one*. John's evidences of authentic spiritual regeneration are thus both inclusive and exclusive. In this way they strengthen the boundaries between those who are truly part of the believing community and those who are not and thus provide a true basis for assurance.

- Authentic Christian faith is always *content full* faith rather than a mere act of believing. The latter is not faith at all but fanaticism. Furthermore, the content of true saving faith is always the Person and Work of Jesus Christ, the Son of God.

- True love for God will always be shown in practice and never be a matter of mere talk or emotion. In particular, love for God will be shown in love for others and obedience to God's commands.

- Faith in Jesus, love for others and obedience to God's commands are all inseparable marks of true regeneration.

- Although we remain sinners, obedience to God's commands is always an encouragement and a joy rather than a burden to the true believer. The true believer is never more joyful than when he or she is walking in willing obedience to God's commands.
- Although we remain sinners in need of daily forgiveness and grace, our faith in Jesus does give us victory over the world. The victorious life is nothing more or less than a life of faith, love and obedience.

Suggestions for preaching

Sermon

The Victorious Christian Life (1 John 5:1-5)

1. Introduction
   - Victorious living – true or false?
2. Everyone who believes…
   - The evidence of faith (5:1)
   - The companions of faith
     - Sincere love for the brothers (5:1)
     - Joyful obedience to God (5:2-3)
   - The victory of faith (5:4-5)
3. Conclusion
   - Victorious life – Normal life!

Suggestions for teaching

Questions to help understand the passage

1. What is the content of authentic Christian faith?

2. Of what is such faith clear evidence?
3. In what way is Christian faith inclusive/exclusive?
4. What will characterise the lives of those who love God? Why must this be so?
5. In what way are love for believers, love for God and obedience to God's commands connected?
6. Why are God's commands not burdensome for believers?
7. What does it mean for the believer to overcome the world?
8. How do believers overcome the world?

Questions to help apply the passage

1. Why is faith in Jesus as the Christ an essential consequence of having been born of God?
2. What is the difference between faith and fanaticism?
3. What effect does regeneration have upon the believer's attitude to obedience to God?
4. How should believers in Christ view God's commands?
5. What does 1 John 5:1-5 teach about the believer's assurance of salvation?
6. What is the victorious Christian life?
7. How does this victorious life become ours?

11
King on the Cross (1 John 5:6-12)

Introduction

Throughout our study of 1 John we have been reminded that John wrote his letter for a definite purpose and within a specific context. The purpose, stated in 1 John 5:13, was to assure his readers that their experience of God's gift of eternal life was indeed genuine since it was authenticated by faith in Jesus Christ, love for their fellow believers, obedience to God and by the inner testimony of God's Holy Spirit. The context of John's letter was the confident and disturbing claims made by a group who had broken both with the community to whom John was writing and with the apostolic gospel which formed the basis of that community's faith and life. At the heart of the teaching of this breakaway group was a clear denial of some fundamental truths, most notably a denial of the truth that the Christ, the Son of God and the man Jesus were and indeed are one and the same person.

It was this denial of the truth about Jesus the Christ and the implications of this denial that gave rise to John's strong counter-claim and testimony about Jesus in 1 John 2:18-27, 4:1-6 and again in 5:6-12, the passage under consideration in this section. According to the secessionists, God's gift of eternal life could be experienced independently of Jesus and of the apostolic testimony about Jesus. According to John, while eternal life is a gift of God, it is a gift which can only be received through faith in Jesus, the Son of God to whom God Himself has borne witness in the Spirit-empowered testimony of John and his fellow eye- and ear-witnesses.

Listening to the text

Context and structure

The declaration that 'only the one who believes that Jesus is the Son of God...overcomes the world' (5:5) leads directly to John's testimony about Jesus: 'this is the One who came...' (5:6). The focus is therefore shifted from the act of believing (5:1-5) to the object of faith, Jesus Christ, the 'One who came by water and blood' (5:6). It is to this Jesus, God's Son the Christ, that God has given testimony (5:7-9) so that whoever believes in Him may have eternal life (5:10-12). Within the passage there is thus a transition from the *object of faith* (Jesus) to the *means of faith* (the testimony of God) to the *outcome of faith* (eternal life).

That the section ends with 5:12 is clear from the re-introduction in 5:13 of the verb 'to write' and the clear statement of purpose in the words 'so that'. The 'these things' which John has written (5:13) refer not merely to the truth about Jesus in 5:6-12 or the teaching that follows in 5:14-21 but to the letter as a whole. Thus 5:13 is the beginning of a new section of the letter, one which concludes the letter with a statement of John's purpose in writing (5:13), a summary of what believers can know with certainty (5:14-20) and a final appeal to the readers to remain steadfast in the face of the deceptive and deadly teaching of the secessionist, a teaching which John identifies not as the truth of God but as idolatry (5:21).

Working through the text

Grammatically, the words 'This is the one who came' in 5:6 refer both to Jesus the Son of God in 5:5 (antecedent) and to Jesus the Christ in 5:6 (complement). This suggests the 'one who came' is to be designated by a combination of the titles that John has already used in the letter, titles which are repeated in 5:6-12. The 'one who came' is thus Jesus the Christ, the Son of God.

What is not nearly as clear and what is thus disputed among commentators is what John meant when he wrote that this one 'came by water and blood' (5:6). The various options are, of course, well summarised in the major commentaries and will not be rehearsed here. Suffice to say that it is not only the 'water and blood' that needs to be explained but also the word 'came', a word that John uses rarely in the letter – twice to speak about the 'coming' of the antichrists (2:18; 4:3) and twice to speak about Jesus the Christ 'having come' (4:2; 5:6).

Given the fact that John only uses the word 'came' twice to speak about the coming of Jesus the Christ, it is preferable to interpret what John means by the coming of Christ in the light of other words that he uses. Here the word 'appeared' is of key importance (1:2; 3:5) as are John's references to the Father having 'sent' His Son (4:9,10,14). John's teaching in these verses can be summed up as follows: In love, the Father *sent* His Son into the world as the Saviour of the world, that is, as an atoning sacrifice for sins so that all who believe in Him might live through Him. In fulfilment of this mission given to Him by His Father, the Son of God *appeared* to take away sin and to destroy the devil's work, thus demonstrating the love that the Father has for us.

Seen in this context, it thus seems preferable to understand the 'coming of Jesus the Christ' 'by water and blood' (5:6) in terms of Jesus' identity and His mission. Although at first glance the phrase by 'water and blood' suggests a single idea, the repetition of the preposition 'by' in the expanded phrase 'He did not come by water only but *by* water and *by* blood' shows that John was referring to two distinguishable, albeit closely connected ideas.

First, what then of the statement that Jesus Christ 'came by water'? The phrase could be taken to be a reference to *purification* by the blood of Jesus (1:7), water thus taken together with blood as a synonym for the death of Jesus (see below). But the phrase 'not by water only' (5:6) suggests a link with the teaching of the secessionists and thus makes a connection between water and the death of Jesus as the Christ unlikely. In my opinion, it is better to see 'water' in connection with the 'anointing' that John refers to in 2:27. There John is referring to the anointing the disciples received from Jesus which remains within them and which teaches them the truth, that is the Holy Spirit. But, as we saw in our discussion of 1 John 2:18-27, this gift of the Spirit comes to every believer from Jesus who is Himself the Christ, the Anointed One. And, as the gospel of John makes clear, it was at His baptism with water by John the Baptist that Jesus was anointed by the Spirit and declared to be the Christ, the One who would baptise His people with the Holy Spirit (see John 1:29-34).

More simply, what did John mean by the statement that Jesus Christ came 'by blood'? Given that the only other reference to blood in the letter is in 1:7: 'the blood of Jesus His Son purifies us from all sin', it is clear that 'blood' in 5:6 must refer to Jesus' death upon the cross. This is in line with John's teaching about the mission of the Son whom 'God sent as an atoning sacrifice for our sins' (4:10) and who thus 'appeared so that He might take away our sins' (3:5). Furthermore, it was precisely as the Christ, the Son of God that Jesus accomplished His Father's saving work on the cross. For John to state that Jesus the Christ 'did not come by water only but by water and by blood' was thus to state that Jesus died as the Christ, that He remained king upon the cross.

Thus by declaring that Jesus the Christ came 'by water and blood' (5:6), John is testifying to the fact that Jesus is indeed the Christ, the Son of God and that the mission which He began in the power of the Spirit at His baptism (*He came by water*) was continued and completed in the power of that same Spirit at the cross (*He came by blood*). Nor could this mission of the Christ, the Son of God have been accomplished without the cross, for His mission concerned atonement for sins and the salvation of the world. Thus, says John, 'He did not come by water only, but by water and blood' (5:6b). Jesus the Son, king both at His baptism and on the cross! As we have already seen and will see again in 5:11-12, it is this Jesus, and this Jesus alone who is to be the true object of saving faith.

Furthermore, it was to the fact that this Jesus was indeed the Christ, the Son of God that God Himself bore testimony in a variety of ways. First, there was the testimony of the Spirit who is the truth (5:6c). I take this to be a reference to Jesus' anointing by the Spirit at His baptism, an event which led John the Baptist, speaking by the Spirit, to testify that Jesus was indeed the Son of God (*cf* John 1:32-34). Man's testimony to Jesus the Christ was thus given greater authority for it came not merely by the word of a man but by revelation from God (5:9). Second, at Jesus' baptism John, speaking with Divine Authority, testified that Jesus the Christ, the one who would baptise with the Spirit, was also the Lamb of God who would take away the sins of the world (*cf* John 1:29). Thus at His baptism, the one who came with water was also identified both by the Spirit and by John the Baptist as the one who would come in blood. In the words of John, 'man's testimony' (5:9), that is the testimony of John the Baptist, made in the power of the Spirit and 'in truth' was confirmed 'both in water and in blood' (5:6), that is, by the baptism and the death of Jesus the Christ. Looking back on these events in the mission of Jesus, John could thus write that as part of God's testimony to His Son Jesus.[1]

(Although the KJV adds a thoroughly Trinitarian statement about the witness in heaven of the Father – the Word and the Spirit at the beginning of verse 7 – the fact that this addition does not have any textual support in manuscripts dating from before the fourteenth century is evidence that it is not original to John but the work of a later scribe. Nor does this addition fit in with John's actual argument in this passage. Indeed, it contradicts it for it presents Jesus as testifying to Himself rather than as the One to whom testimony is born. I have thus respectfully omitted it from the commentary.)

---

1. 'There are three that testify: the Spirit, the water and the blood; and the three are in agreement' (1 John 5:7-8).

There is, however, something more that needs to be said concerning this testimony of the Sprit, the water, the blood and the testimony of God the Father. The events to which we have made reference above all lay in the past when John wrote. Together then they made up the testimony that 'God has given about His Son' (5:9). In what sense could they then be said to 'testify' (present tense) to John's readers? The answer is surely found in the opening paragraph of the letter. For in that opening paragraph John reminds his readers that what took place in the past, in the history of Jesus the Christ, was proclaimed by those who had seen and heard and touched, so that later generations may also see and hear and believe. In the words of 1 John 1:2-3 'the life appeared; we have seen it and testify to it, and we proclaim to you the eternal life which was with the Father and has appeared to us. We proclaim to you what we have seen and heard so that you also may have fellowship with us. And our fellowship is with the Father and with His Son Jesus Christ'. In declaring that Jesus Christ came both by water and blood, John was thus proclaiming God's own testimony about His Son Jesus so that his readers might also believe (*cf* John 20:30-31).

By believing the testimony of John, the readers thus believed what God Himself had testified concerning Jesus His Son (5:10). In that way, and in that way alone, they had received the gift of eternal life which is to be found only in Jesus the Christ, the Son of God (5:11). John 's reference to the first 'whoever' in 5:10a and 5:12a thus served once more to assure and encourage his readers that they did indeed possess the eternal life that Jesus gives and that through Jesus they did indeed truly know God.

By contrast, those who rejected John's testimony about Jesus also rejected the testimony that God had given to His

Son. Refusal to believe in this Jesus, who came by water and blood and not by water only, thus made God out to be a liar (5:10). And since eternal life is found in Jesus, the Son of God, and in Him alone, refusal to believe God's testimony to Jesus given by those who had seen and heard, meant (and continues to mean) the rejection of the life that He alone could give. In John's words: 'This is the testimony: God has given us eternal life and this life is in His Son. Whoever has the Son has life; whoever does not have the Son does not have life' (5:11-12). Just as the first 'whoever' functioned as an encouragement for John's readers, the second 'whoever' (5:10b; 5:12b) stood as a warning to them not to listen to the teaching of the secessionists and so be drawn away from the life which is in Christ. As we shall see below, this theme of assurance and warning continues in the final section of the letter.

From text to message

John's declaration that Jesus the Christ came 'both by water and by blood' is a timely reminder that any view of the kingship of Jesus which fails to affirm the centrality of the cross is not only flawed but spiritually destructive. And yet such views of the kingship of Jesus continue to be taught today, not least by those who have wandered away from the truth and who seek to draw others away as well. Despite this tragic state of affairs, God's own testimony to His Son stands true, a testimony confirmed by God Himself through His Word and in the power of His Spirit. It is a testimony which every Christian should not only accept personally and wholeheartedly but also maintain in a world which is in deep need of the eternal life that only Jesus can offer. As we noted in the previous section, the world and the worldly church has little time for absolute statements about God or Jesus. In such a world there is no place for truth. But, as John reminds us in 5:6, it is in the final analysis 'the Spirit who testifies because the Spirit is the truth'. Our task is thus to faithfully proclaim what the Spirit affirmed about Jesus the Christ – that He the Christ, the Son of God, is this Christ upon the cross and that, therefore, by His death, He is the one who grants eternal life to all who put their trust in Him. It is this central message that we must be sure to communicate as we teach a passage which is not easy to interpret but which is vital to understand.

Getting the message clear: the theme

Jesus who was anointed as the Christ, the Son of God, at His baptism remained king throughout His mission and especially in His death upon the cross. It is only by faith in this Jesus who died that we receive God's gift of eternal life.

Getting the message clear: the aim

- To affirm that Jesus as proclaimed in the apostolic gospel is indeed the Christ, the Son of God and that eternal life is to be found in Him alone.
- To encourage those who have put their faith in this Jesus to continue to trust in Him.

A way in

One way in is to reflect on the fact that throughout history there have been those who, while happy to refer to Jesus as King, have objected to his atoning death upon the cross as the true and final expression of His kingship. Down the ages there have been those who have echoed the words: 'Let this Christ, this King of Israel, come down now from the cross that we may see and believe' (Mark 15:32). The gospels agree that at His baptism, Jesus was anointed by the Spirit and acknowledged by God as His King. Jesus' baptism thus began his public ministry as the Christ of God. But the gospels also agree that it was precisely as King that Jesus was crucified and so doing accomplished His great saving work for the people of God. At baptism and on the cross, by water and by blood, Jesus is thus seen and declared to be King, the one and only Son of God through whom we can have life.

Ideas for application

- John's insistence that Jesus came by water *and* blood reminds us of the essential nature of the death of Jesus. Without the cross, Jesus' kingship is ineffectual.
- God's testimony to the authority of Jesus the Messiah, given in history by the Spirit and in His baptism and death, is still the basis of our faith today.
- God's testimony to His Son Jesus comes to us via the testimony of John and the other eyewitnesses to Jesus' ministry.
- The truth about Jesus can thus only be known via the apostolic gospel. It is by believing this gospel that we enter into life giving relationship with Jesus God's Son.
- Only those who put their faith in Jesus Christ and Him the crucified One have eternal life.
- Everyone who believes in Jesus Christ and Him the crucified One does have life.

Suggestions for preaching

Sermon

King on the Cross (1 John 5:6-12)

1. Introduction
    - Jesus as the King – a familiar melody
    - King on the Cross – a jarring note
2. The Object of our faith
    - Jesus the Anointed King
    - Jesus the Dying King
3. The Means of our faith
    - The testimony of man
    - The testimony of God
4. The Outcome of our faith
    - Whoever believes...
    - Whoever does not believe...
5. Conclusion
    - Only one way!

Suggestions for teaching

Questions to help understand the passage

1. To whom does the phrase 'this is the one who came' refer?
2. What titles does John use to describe this 'one who came'?

3. According to John, how did Jesus the Christ, the Son of God come?

4. Who/what testifies to the fact that Jesus is indeed the Christ, the Son of God?

5. In what way does man's testimony and God's testimony to His Son work together?

6. What testimony has God given about His Son?

7. Why is it essential to believe the testimony which God has given about His Son?

Questions to help apply the passage

1. How can we know from this passage that what John has written about Jesus is the truth?

2. What key truths are we to believe about Jesus if we are to have eternal life?

3. What does this passage say to those who reject the death of Jesus as central to his mission as God's king?

4. What does this passage say to those who claim that there are other ways to spiritual life apart from faith in Jesus Christ?

5. In what ways does this passage challenge prevailing views about Christianity?

6. In what way does this passage strengthen the assurance of those who believe in Jesus?

12

THAT YOU MAY KNOW...
(1 JOHN 5:13-21)

Introduction

In this final section we focus on John's conclusion to his letter. A conclusion that begins with a statement of his purpose for writing (5:13) and that ends with an urgent appeal to his readers to remain steadfast in the face of the deceptive and, thus, deadly teaching of the false prophets who have broken away from the gospel and thus from the believing community. A teaching which claimed to lead to a deeper knowledge and experience of God but which was in reality nothing other than idolatry (5:21).

As we would expect from a conclusion, much of the paragraph is familiar from the letter as a whole and is therefore relatively easy to understand. Thus John speaks about assurance and its immediate benefit, namely confidence in prayer as an expression of true fellowship with God (5:13-15; *cf* 3:21-22). He speaks about the keeping power of Christ which enables the believer to overcome the world and to resist the wiles of the devil, especially as these are manifested in the teaching of the secessionists (5:18-19;

cf 4:1-6). And he speaks about the inner certainty that all who know Jesus Christ have concerning the truth and the life that are found only in Him (5:20; *cf* 2:20).

In the midst of these familiar themes we also find a much more difficult section in which John distinguishes 'sin that does not lead to death' from 'sin that leads to death' (5:16-17) and gives advice regarding prayer for those who seem to be in danger of straying away from the life which is found only in Jesus. But even in this regard it is important to remember that John is unlikely to introduce anything new at the end of the letter and that his teaching about sin, life and death are simply a summary in urgent and thus stark terms of what he has already taught elsewhere in the letter. Just what these particular sins are, why John mentions them at this point in the letter and in this particular way and what their precise link is with John's closing exhortation to his readers is, of course, a matter for more detailed comment in the discussion that follows.

Listening to the text

Context and structure

As is the case with the fourth Gospel, 1 John ends with an explicit statement by John regarding his purpose for writing. Reflecting back upon the letter as a whole, John states that he 'wrote these things' (i.e. the letter) so that those who believe in the name of the Son of God *may know that they have eternal life* (5:13). Thus a letter that began with the proclamation of the eternal life which appeared so that those who believe may have the joy of fellowship with God through His Son Jesus Christ (1:3-4) ends by assuring those who believe that they do indeed have this life and that the fellowship that they enjoy with the Father in the name of His Son Jesus is truly authentic.

One might in fact have expected 1 John 5:13 to be the final verse in the letter, but given what we know about the threat that faced John's readers, it is not surprising to find that John follows his statement of purpose with a series of statements that serve both to affirm what the believers in Jesus do indeed have and know and to exhort them not only to stand firm themselves but to take responsibility for the spiritual well-being of others within the community. In a letter which urges its readers to continue in Christ and to love one another this is only to be expected.

Traditionally this final passage of the letter is divided into three subsections, namely 5:13-15, 5:16-17 and 5:18-21. For our purposes we will divide it into an opening statement of purpose (5:13) linked to a closing exhortation (5:21), an affirmation about the confidence that believers can have in prayer and an application of that confidence in regard to prayer for those who are in danger of being led astray (5:14-17), and a re-affirmation of the keeping power of Christ and the assurance that every believer can have in the light of this fact (5:18-20).

Working through the text

Opening statement and closing exhortation (5:13 and 5:21). As we noted above, the passage begins with a final reference to John's act of writing and a clear statement of the purpose for which he wrote (5:13). The use of the past tense 'wrote' is in keeping with John's practice in the second part of the letter, beginning in 2:14. Its use in 5:13 in conjunction with a statement of purpose is, however, particularly striking and underlines the fact that the letter itself is part of John's testimony to the truth about Jesus, intended as a witness to the truth for successive generations of readers. As John looks back upon his work, he can assure his readers that it is his testimony rather than the boastful claims of the secessionists which will provide a sure foundation for their relationship with God.

On the previous occasions where he has made specific reference to his writing, John has often added a personal form of address such as 'dear children' (2:1,12,14) or 'dear friends' (2:7-8). In our discussion of these verses we noted that John's use of these forms of address was to remind his readers of his affectionate and committed relationship with them and so doing to encourage them to take his teaching to heart. In 5:13, John refers to his readers in more objective yet no less significant terms.

Those to whom he has addressed his letter are specifically the ones who 'believe in the name of the Son of God'. Once again the tense of the verb (present tense) is significant and serves as a reminder to John's readers that saving faith in Jesus must remain an ongoing reality if they are to remain in life giving fellowship with God through Christ (*cf* John's appeal to his readers to 'remain' or 'continue' in Christ in 2:24-28). Furthermore, John refers to his readers as those who believe in the 'name' of the Son of God. Here he is once more drawing from earlier teaching for in 2:12 he reminded his readers that their sins had been 'forgiven on account of his name' and in 3:23 he reminded them of God's command 'to believe in the name of His Son, Jesus Christ'. As John has made clear throughout his letter and in particular at the end of the previous section (*cf* 5:11-12), only those who have believed and who continue to believe in the name of Jesus, the Son of God have eternal life and it is to them in particular that John has addressed his letter so that they may be assured and confident in their relationship with God.

But as we have also seen throughout the letter, John's affirmation of his readers in their faith in Christ is never seen as grounds for presumption. Those who believe in Christ are also exhorted to remain in Christ so that they may be confident and unashamed at his coming (*cf* 2:28). And this exhortation to remain was of particular importance given the deceptive teaching of those whom John had labelled as antichrists and false prophets. As with the false prophets of old, their teaching, though appealing in its worldliness (*cf* 4:5) and though presented as a superior form of spirituality, did not in fact lead toward the knowledge of God but away from it. John had already pointed this out in a number of different ways in his letter, but in his final exhortation to his readers, he states this in stark terms. For John the teaching of the secessionists was in fact not truth but error, teaching which led not to the knowledge of God but to the worship of idols (5:21). Having thus assured his readers of their relationship with God in Christ, he warns them not to fall for a deceptive and false alternative no matter how impressive it may appear. And it is here, in this firm warning, that the personal form of address appears for a final time in the letter. It is because of his love for his readers and his burden for their eternal well-being that he not only assures them but warns them as his dear children to keep themselves from the idolatry of false teaching and a worldly way of life.

Confidence in prayer and concern for those who sin (5:14-17)
That assurance of salvation should and does lead to confidence in a believer's relationship with the Lord and has

already been clearly taught in 1 John. As we have seen, the word is used twice to speak of the 'confidence' that the believer in Jesus Christ can have with respect to the day of judgement when Christ returns (*cf* 2:28; 4:17). It is with a view to this confidence that John calls upon his readers to remain in Christ (*cf* 2:24,28). The word is also used twice to speak about the confidence that believers enjoy in their daily walk with the Lord and, in particular, in prayer. In 3:21-22, John reminds his readers that those who belong to the truth can 'set their hearts at rest in his presence' since the Lord is 'greater than our hearts' (3:19,20 NIV and KJV). Having set their hearts at rest, believers can then have confidence that they will receive from God anything they ask. It is this particular confidence before the Lord in prayer that is once again in view in 5:14-15, though in the latter verses the 'anything' of 3:22 is qualified by the words 'according to his will' (5:14 NIV and KJV). There is no contradiction, however, because even in 3:22 the 'anything' was to be understood in terms of what pleases the Lord and is in obedience to His commands (see 3:22-24). John's point in both cases is that the believer in Christ can approach God confidently in prayer because such an approach is based upon a true relationship with God through Christ. In such a relationship God always hears and always answers the prayers of His people (5:15) in accordance with His will for them and for their eternal good.

In the context of 1 John 5:14-17 and of the letter as a whole, the particular prayer that is in view is the prayer for a brother who has committed 'a sin which does not lead to death' (5:16). That no believer is 'without sin' and that all believers do in fact sin was, as we noted in our discussion of 1:5-2:2, one of the fundamental points of disagreement between John and the secessionists. It is, of course, not that

John was ambivalent about sin (*cf* 2:1; 3:7-10), but he was realistic about sin and concerned that none of his readers be misled by the secessionists on this matter. John was, however, equally clear that the true believer must and, indeed, would have a desire to walk in the light (1:7) and to live as Jesus did (2:6), seeking by the power of the Spirit to live a life of love for one another and of obedience to God's commands (3:4-10). This way of life – the life of forgiven sinners who are committed to living by faith in Jesus Christ, with love for one another and in obedience to God – is, in my opinion, what John is referring to when he speaks of living life in fellowship with God and with one another. This way of life is thus the way of eternal life in and through Jesus Christ. It is the life of a sinner, yes, but not of 'sin that leads to death'.

If this is so, then a refusal to accept and follow this way of life, by rejecting Christ, refusing to love one another and refusing to obey God's words is surely the life of 'continuing to sin' (3:9; 5:18), a way of life that shows that a person is not born of God and devoid of God's seed of life within them. It is this way of life that John has in mind when he speaks about 'sin that leads to death' (5:16b); the way of life of a sinner whose sins remain unforgiven because of their rejection of the One in whose name alone all sin can be forgiven and eternal life received. It is, of course, true that many reject Christ and live in rebellion against God, but in this context John has the secessionists, in particular, in mind. Although John does not forbid his readers from praying for these people, he does not enjoin it (5:16). Indeed there is nothing in the letter at all to suggest that it is God's will that these false prophets and antichrists should or would repent.

What about those who commit sin that does not lead to death? As we noted above and as John says in 5:17, 'all wrongdoing is sin, and there is sin that does not lead to death'. Though believers continue to struggle against a sinful nature, they are also through Christ continually able to confess their sins and be purified from unrighteousness (*cf* 1:9). The fact that they do sin, does not cause them to be cut off from the eternal life that God gives to those who trust in Christ. But it is important that sin is dealt with and not allowed to become a pattern for life. It is precisely with this in mind that John writes to the community of forgiven sinners 'if you see any brother or sister commit a sin that does not lead to death, you should pray' (5:16).

Love for the brothers will thus mean a commitment to pray for one another that the sin that inevitably happens will not harden into stubborn-hearted rebellion; that our love for the Lord and His people will not be choked by a love for the world; that our commitment to truth will not be undermined by the teaching of those who preach another, easier gospel, a gospel which seeks life apart from the way of the cross. Unlike Cain (3:12), the true believer *is* his brother's keeper. Although perseverance in the faith is a personal responsibility, it cannot be done in one's own strength. In order to persevere in the faith, the believer needs the fellowship of other believers and the keeping power of God to be at work. It is this keeping power that John has in mind when he speaks about God 'giving life' to a brother in answer to the prayer of a fellow believer. The eternal life which is ours as a gift from God will only be ours in fullness when Christ appears. For John, therefore, eternal life is thus both a present gift (5:13) and a future promise (2:25). The key for the believer who has life is to remain in the Son and in the Father (2:24) and this can only happen through God's life-giving power at work day by day and through the keeping power of the Son of God, the very power that John speaks about in the next verse.

Blessed Assurance (5:18-20)

In these verses which lead to John's final exhortation the believer's assurance is once again in view. Three times John uses the phrase 'we know' to underline the believer's sure and certain knowledge, knowledge which is fundamental to a life of faith, love and obedience in the midst of a fallen and hostile world.

First, says John, 'we know that anyone born of God does not continue to sin: the One born of God keeps them safe and the evil one cannot harm them' (5:18). The previous concern for the perseverance of every believer does not mean that John has no confidence in the keeping power of God. The 'one born of God' is Jesus, God's eternal Son and it is He who sustains the life of the believer enabling them to withstand the attack of the evil one, an attack launched, of course, through the deceptive but deadly teaching of the secessionists. In 2:13-14, John encouraged his readers that they had indeed 'overcome the evil one', having been forgiven in the name of Jesus and thus knowing Him who was from the beginning. Here he reminds them that the one who forgave them is the one who keeps them safe to the very end.

Second, says John, 'we know that we are children of God (*lit.* 'of God') and that the whole world is under the control of the evil one (*lit.* lies in the evil one)' (5:19). In this statement John draws a clear demarcation between two and only two groups. On the one hand are those who are 'of God' i.e. born of God and thus children of God (*cf* 3:1-9) among whom are John's readers. On the other hand there is the world, including in particular, the secessionists who are 'from the world and who speak from the viewpoint of the world' (*cf* 4:5). John's point in 5:19 is that who are from the world and who speak from the world are in fact from the devil, even though they may claim to be from God and to speak for God. Thus John is once again assuring his readers of their true standing in God and urging them to resist the influence of the secessionists.

Third and finally, says John, 'we know that the Son of God has come and that He has given us understanding' (5:20). The verbs 'come' and 'has given' both speak of past events with present consequences. First, in keeping with His Father's mission, the Son of God 'has come' into the world in flesh and as such, He was proclaimed by those who saw and heard Him (1:1-2). Second, the Son of God came to John's readers through the proclamation of the gospel 'in the beginning' and in the power of the Spirit, the anointing, who made the truth about God's Son known to them (*cf* 2:20-27). Thus by the Spirit the Son of God has given 'understanding' to believers so that they 'may know the truth' (5:20b). But, as the remainder of the verse makes clear and in contrast to the teaching of secessionists, to know this truth and to have this understanding is not a matter of abstract philosophical or spiritual 'knowledge'. To know the truth is (*lit.*) to be 'in the truth, in His Son Jesus Christ' (5:20c). For John true spiritual knowledge is thus neither more nor less than a living relationship with Jesus Christ because (*lit.*) 'He is the true God and the eternal life' (5:20d). Thus at the end of the letter John again affirms the message that has been proclaimed from the beginning. The eternal life that was with the Father has appeared in the person of Jesus Christ. To have the Son is thus to know God and to have life; not to have the Son is however not to have life and far from knowing God, is to have fallen prey to the deadly sin of idolatry. This brings the reader quite naturally to the urgent warning in 5:21 with which the letter ends.

From text to message

Although 1 John 5:13-21 is short enough to deal with in a single talk, it is probably better to deal with the passage in a short series. This allows the opportunity not only to unravel some of the more difficult sections such as 5:16-17, but also to summarise and reinforce the teaching of the letter as a whole. The opening verse makes it absolutely clear that the assurance of those who believe in Jesus Christ is the main concern of the passage, as it is of the entire letter. Thus as one deals with each sub-section it is important to keep this primary theme in mind.

In the commentary above, I have sought in particular to link 5:13 and 5:21. In my opinion this link is very important, for taken in isolation 5:21 can either be viewed as an after thought or as the key verse to the whole. In my opinion, neither of these approaches does justice to the verse as it stands in context. Reading 5:13 and 5:21 together focusses our attention on John's main point in the letter, namely, to assure his readers of the authenticity of their faith in a context in which that faith is being challenged by an alternative and spurious theology. The intervening material simply summarises, underlines and applies John's teaching with this particular goal in mind.

Getting the message clear: the theme

Those who believe in Jesus the Christ, the Son of God are the ones who truly have eternal life. Therefore, every believer must not only continue in this life of faith with the help of Christ's keeping power but also prayerfully encourage their fellow believers to persevere as well.

Getting the message clear: the aim

- To assure believers in Jesus Christ the Son of God that they do indeed have eternal life.
- To encourage believers to persevere in their faith in Christ, notwithstanding the many alternatives views that are presented.
- To urge believers to pray for and to encourage their fellow believers to persevere in their faith in Christ and daily walk with Him.

A way in

Given the summary nature of the passage and its role as the conclusion of the letter, one way in to a short series on this passage could be to look back over the past talks and to remind the hearers of John's primary aim in writing and our primary goal in studying 1 John. If, as I have suggested above, one deals with 5:13 and 5:21 together, then a way in might be to start with 5:21 and to ask the hearers why they think that John has ended his letter with this verse. This could lead to an opening point about John's striking definition of false theology as idolatry.

A way in to talk 2 in the series could be to remind the readers of the importance that John gives to brotherly love as a fundamental part of discipleship. Although brotherly love is to be shown in different ways, it is nowhere more important than when it is directed to encouragement and prayer for our fellow believers, especially those who are struggling. In 5:14-17, John reminds us that the assurance and confidence we have is to be enjoyed by all believers and to be applied in the care of others as well as our own joy and fulfilment.

A way into talk 3 is to speak about the way in which the New Testament views the world and the clear distinction that it draws between those who belong to God and those who do not. John thus presents us not so much with two ways to live as the one and only way to live. The alternative is the way of death. The dividing line within humanity is not class, race, gender or socio-economic status but faith in Jesus who is God's only way to life.

Ideas for application

- Since faith in Jesus is the result of and thus evidence for regeneration, every believer can and should enjoy assurance of salvation.
- Assurance of salvation gives the believer confidence in approaching God in prayer.
- It is God's will and an expression of love for one another to pray for fellow believers and for their perseverance in the faith.
- The only sin that makes salvation impossible is rebellion against Jesus Christ and the salvation that He alone can bring. Rejection of Jesus the Christ, the Son of God is thus sin that leads to death.
- Believers in Jesus remain in fellowship with God despite the fact that they are sinners. Not all sin is sin that leads to death.
- The true believer is taught the truth by God's Holy Spirit and has come to understand that

eternal life can be found only in Jesus the Christ, the Son of God.

Suggestions for preaching

Sermon 1

Encouragement and Exhortation (5:13 & 5:21)

1. Introduction
    - Looking back
    - That we may know....
2. 5:21 – A striking ending
    - A text to be read in context
    - Idolatrous Christianity?
        - False theology, worldly Christianity
    - Keep yourself from idols!
3. 5:13 – An empowering assurance
    - The power of the Name
    - The certainty of faith

Sermon 2

Confident Prayer (5:14-17)

1. Introduction
    - Bold we approach
    - Am I my brother's keeper?
2. Life, Sin and Death
    - The sin that leads to death

- The sin of those who live
- Prayer for life

3. Conclusion – Loving a sinful brother
    - If you see
    - Care enough to pray

Sermon 3
Assured Knowledge (5:18-20)

1. Introduction
    - Two ways to live?
    - A world divided
2. The Knowledge that leads to life
    - Safe in the hands of Jesus
    - Children of God
    - Knowing Him who is the truth
3. Conclusion
    - He is the true God
    - He is eternal life
    - Life by knowing Him

Suggestions for teaching

Questions to help understand the passage

1. To whom is John's letter primarily addressed?
2. What is meant by 'these things' in 5:13?

3. What is the definition of a Christian according to 5:13?
4. Why did John write his letter?
5. What two things can the believer be confident about in prayer?
6. What two kinds of sin does John distinguish? What is the difference between them?
7. According to John, how should a believer respond to sin within the community?
8. In this context, what does it mean for God to 'give life' to a brother who sins?
9. According to 5:18-20 what three things can the believer know?
10. What does 5:20 teach us about the Person of Jesus?
11. What word does John use to describe the false belief and way of life of the secessionists?

Questions to help apply the passage

1. What do we learn about assurance from 5:13?
2. Why is assurance important for every Christian?
3. In what way does assurance before God assist our confidence in prayer?
4. How should believers respond to sin within the believing community? Why should we respond this way?
5. Are we obligated to pray for the repentance of false teachers? What is the reason for your answer?

6. What does this passage teach us about sin in the life of the believer?
7. Why can believers in Jesus have assurance that they will persevere?
8. How does this assurance encourage personal perseverance?
9. What perspective should we have on the world and our identity within the world?
10. What does this passage teach about the Person of Jesus?
11. What does this passage say to the objection that as Christians we cannot have certainty in the faith?

Part 3
Teaching 2 John

I
The Fellowship of Love and Truth (2 John 1-3)

Introduction

As we noted in the general introduction to John's letters, 2 John has all the characteristics of a first century letter. It has the customary address identifying both sender and recipients, in this case, 'the elder' and 'the chosen lady and her children' (v. 1). It contains the customary greeting and benediction, expressed in typically Christian terms ('grace, mercy and peace' – v. 3). And it ends with a concluding paragraph expressing the writer's desire to see the readers 'face to face' (v. 12) and communicating final greetings (v. 13). And, as is the case in particular with letters in the New Testament, each of these formal elements of the standard letter have been elaborated and expanded to introduce and emphasise the writer's main concerns and ultimate purpose for writing. As we shall see below, these elaborations are of key importance for our interpretation of the letter, both in its own terms and as part of the Johannine epistolary corpus.

Listening to the text

Context and structure

Although the themes of 'love' and 'truth' which are introduced in the opening verse of the letter continue into verses 4-5, the traditional pattern: Sender–recipients–greeting makes it clear that verses 1-3 form a single unit serving to introduce the letter. The play on the words 'love' and 'truth' is clear as is the close connection between the two. In verse 1 the writer speaks about his relationship with the readers as one of 'love in the truth' while in verse 3 the order of the words is reversed to 'in truth and love'. A central affirmation, providing the basis of the writer's close and confident relationship with the readers, speaks simply of 'the truth' (v. 2), but the link with 'love' is maintained by the preposition 'because'. This central affirmation also makes it clear that wherever the word 'truth' is used it is '*the* truth' rather than the more general noun 'truth' or the adverb 'truly' that is in view. As we shall see, this is of particular importance when it comes to the writer's exhortation in verses 8-11.

Working through the text

The letter begins with a simple title identifying the writer as 'the elder'. This title, used again in 3 John 1, strongly suggests a common authorship of both of these epistles, but also raises the question whether the elder responsible for 2 and 3 John is to be identified with the author of 1 John and indeed with the author of the Fourth Gospel. As we noted in the General Introduction to John's letters, there is no compelling reason to doubt the common authorship of all three letters or to reject the traditional view that the author of 1-3 John was indeed the Apostle John, the author of the Fourth Gospel. Certainly the links between 2 John and 1 John are strong, both in relation to theme and provenance, and given the common title 'elder' in 2 John 1 and 3 John 1, the close connection between all three seems well established. Indeed, as we shall see below, 2 and 3 John are connected thematically as well, even though the recipients are different.

Why then the self-designation 'the elder' on the part of the writer? Although it is possible to speculate, the simple answer must be that this was the title by which the writer of the letter was known to his readers. In its own terms the title suggests both authority and relationship, both of which are clearly evident in the opening paragraph and in the letter as a whole.

Although the letter is written from within a community, the writer speaks not merely on behalf of fellow believers (v. 1; *cf* v. 13) but in his own right (v. 1; *cf* v. 12). It is clear that he views his readers with deep affection within a strong relationship based around a common commitment to the truth (v. 1-2) and that he expects his future meeting with them to be one which is marked by joyful fellowship in this same truth (v. 12). But it is also clear that he expects his readers to take what he says to heart, to heed his warnings (v. 8) and to act upon his instructions (vv. 5, 10). All of this is precisely what one would expect from the relationship between an elder and the congregation over whom he exercises care and authority. The fact that the writer is located at a distance from the congregation, thus necessitating a letter and a visit, does not in itself detract from this relationship. On the contrary, it merely suggests that the writer's position within the wider Christian community was a significant one and that the readers held him in high regard. As we noted in §1, this is consistent with the writer being identified with the Apostle John, who according to early but venerable tradition had particular responsibility for congregations within Asia Minor, especially those around Ephesus.

From the 'elder' we turn our attention to the recipients of the letter whom the writer describes as 'the chosen lady and her children' (v. 1 NASB). It is best to view the 'lady' and 'her children' as terms denoting the same group of people, namely the faithful members of a local congregation. This is confirmed first by the writer's alternating use of the second person singular (vv. 4,5,13) and the second person plural pronoun (vv. 6,8,10,12) to refer to his readers and in verse 13 where the writer sends greetings from 'the children of your sister who is chosen', here clearly a single, inclusive group. What is more significant is the elder's description of the congregation to whom he writes as the 'elect' (KJV) ('chosen by God' NIV). Although the noun 'God' is not there in the original, it is implied, thus reminding the congregation of the privileged position it holds as well as the responsibility it bears. As we shall see, a clear grasp of both this privilege and this responsibility will be of the utmost importance as the congregation is called to deal with the threat of missionary preachers whose progressive teaching is not a step forward in spiritual growth but a pathway away from the truth.

Having identified himself and reminded his hearers of their privileged position as those chosen by God, the elder now describes his relationship with his readers as one characterised by 'love in *the* truth' (v. 1), not merely 'love in truth'. Although the word 'truth' does not have the definite article in this phrase, the two-fold presence of the definite article in the remainder of the sentence ('know *the* truth' (v. 1) and 'because of *the* truth' (v. 2)), makes it clear that the definite article must be supplied in this initial instance as well. The elder is not saying that he 'truly loves' those to whom he is writing, but that his love for them is 'in the truth'. Indeed, as he makes clear, his love for them is not only 'in the truth', but arises 'because of the truth'. Thus the relationship he has with his readers is both initiated and sustained by the truth.

What is this truth that the elder values so highly? The answer to this question is found in what follows in the letter, particularly in the orthodox confession of the 'teaching of Christ' (v. 9), that is, the acknowledgement that 'Jesus Christ has come in the flesh' (v. 7). In the introduction to the letter, however, the elder describes it in a number of striking ways. First, it is truth that can be and is *known* by all believers (v. 1). Second, it is *indwelling truth* (v. 2), truth that 'lives in' all true believers. Third, it is *eternal truth* (v. 2), truth that 'will be with us forever'. For the elder, the truth is not dead orthodoxy, but vital, life-giving truth. This is precisely what he has in mind when he links this 'truth' with the 'grace, mercy and peace' that come from 'God the Father and from Jesus Christ the Father's Son' (v. 3).

The benediction 'grace, mercy and peace' is found only here in John's letters. Furthermore, it differs from the normal New Testament epistolary benedictions in that it is not a prayer but a declaration. According to the elder, all who are chosen by God the Father are already and will continue to be the recipients of the Father's 'grace, mercy and peace' (v. 3). Here as elsewhere in the New Testament 'grace' is a reference to 'unmerited favour' and 'mercy', a reference to God's acts toward His people as a result of His grace, most notably the forgiveness of their sins. Used in conjunction with 'grace' and 'mercy', 'peace' is then in all likelihood not a subjective sense of the peace of God, but the reality of 'peace with God', i.e. reconciliation and renewed fellowship with God. Furthermore, and in keeping with the central theme of all of John's letters, this experience of the 'grace, mercy and peace' which comes from God the Father also comes 'from Jesus Christ' (v. 3). Without Jesus the Christ, no one can or will enjoy the reality of God's 'grace, mercy and peace' which are the expression of God's love for His people.

But this 'grace, mercy and peace' which are with believers 'in love', that is, as the expression of the love of God for them (v. 3), is also theirs 'in truth', that is as a result of 'the truth'. This truth, the truth about Jesus the Father's Son, is what joins believers to the Son and thus to the Father. This of course raises the question of how this truth about Jesus came to the believers in the first place. As we shall see, this truth came to the believers via 'the teaching of Christ' (v. 9) which they heard from the beginning (vv. 5,6), teaching in which they were called to remain, despite the appeals of a new group of messengers who had come with a 'progressive' but fundamentally flawed message (v. 10). Grace, mercy and peace thus came to the believers in and through 'the truth' found in Christ, truth heard and believed through the teaching of the true gospel of which the elder was the authorised spokesman.

One final observation must be made about this opening paragraph and that is to note the link that the elder draws between 'the truth' and 'love'. As we have seen, the elder's relationship with his fellow believers and their relationship with each other is described as 'love in the truth' and 'love because of the truth' (vv. 1,2). The benediction of God the Father and of Jesus Christ the Son comes to believers 'in truth and love' (v. 3). For the elder truth and love are not only both of key importance, they are also inseparable from one another. As we shall see this fact is the basis of the elder's exhortation in verses 4-6 and his warning and instruction in verses 7-11.

From text to message

Although 2 John has a very clear and particular historical context, the fact that it is part of the New Testament means that it comes to us not merely as an object of historical interest but as the very Word of God to His church today. Indeed, every local congregation of believers in every age can be described as the 'chosen lady and her children'. This means, of course, that the elder's exhortation to his original readers remains his exhortation to the church today and thus that the particular themes that he emphasises in the introductory greeting and benediction should be carefully noted and considered. This is particularly true when it comes to the repeated emphasis both in this passage and in the next that *both* truth *and* love matter in the life of the individual believer and of the congregation.

As we shall see, the purpose of 2 John was to encourage discernment among the readers, in particular with regard to the welcome and support of visiting preachers. The elder's concern was not that his readers should balance love against truth, but rather that they should express the right kind of love, namely 'love in truth', rather than empty and gullible sentimentality. This kind of sentimental approach to teachers and teaching is sadly still rife within the church today. In this context, we need to be reminded that though love matters, it must never be separated from truth. Indeed, to do so is to be out of step not only with the elder whose love is 'in the truth' but with God Himself whose ultimate act of love was demonstrated in the One who Himself was and is 'the Truth'.

Getting the message clear: the theme

The relationship of love that exists between believers and believing congregations will only be an authentic and God-honouring relationship if it is based on the truth about Jesus. Among God's true elect *both* love *and* truth are of importance.

Getting the message clear: the aim

To establish the vital link between love and truth in the life of every believer and each believing congregation.

A way in

One way in is to point out that in our own day a commitment to tolerance and acceptance is far more prevalent than a commitment to truth. In such a society, where everyone's view is valid, and where intolerance seems to be the unpardonable sin, discernment is in short supply. In such a world, the call for discernment is easily denounced as judgmentalism. And yet we also live in a world in which religion has become a tool for the manipulation and control of the undiscerning and in which the charlatan and the false prophet are familiar figures. Surely in such a world a renewed call for discernment is of the utmost importance. Where can the balance be found? The answer surely must lie in the elder's clear teaching that love and truth are two inseparable and vital elements of an authentic spiritual life.

Ideas for application

- All believers can be described as 'chosen by God'.
- All believers share in the blessings of the Father that come to us in Jesus Christ.
- Love and truth are inseparable and essential aspects of the life of the believer.

- Love and truth must be kept together in our dealings with others within the believing community.
- The grace, mercy and peace of God in which all believers do share are ours only in and through Jesus Christ.

Suggestions for preaching

Sermon

A Peculiar People (2 John 1-3)

1. Introduction
   - A Tolerant World
   - A Confused World
2. The Lady and her children
   - Chosen by God
   - Loved in and because of the truth
   - A community of love and the truth
   - Blessed by God in love and truth

Suggestions for teaching

Questions to help understand the passage

1. How does the writer refer to himself?
2. What is there in the letter which gives us a clue to his reason behind this title?
3. How does the writer refer to his readers?

4. In what way does the elder describe his relationship with his readers?
5. In what way are love and truth connected in this passage?
6. How did God's grace, mercy and peace come to the readers?
7. What title does the writer give to Jesus?
8. In what way does this passage show the equality between the Father and the Son?

Questions to help apply the passage

1. In what way does this passage highlight the privileges that believers in Jesus enjoy?
2. In what way are love and truth connected in the Christian community?
3. How is the truth formative of authentic Christian experience and community?
4. Why is it important to keep both love and truth together in our relationships as believers?

2
Walking in Truth and Love (2 John 4-6)

Introduction

In the introductory paragraph, the elder took the opportunity to renew his relationship with his readers and to remind them that among the people of God both love and the truth are of the utmost importance. He reminded them of their privileged position as a people chosen by God and blessed in the Lord Jesus Christ with a saving experience of the 'grace, mercy and peace' of God. As a believing community they were by God's grace thus a community of 'truth and love'. In the next section of the letter (vv. 4-6), the elder's goal is to affirm and to exhort his readers, reminding them of their responsibility to remain committed both to truth and to love, not least in their relationship with himself and his associates. As we shall see in our study of verses 7-11, the context for that reminder was the risk posed by a group of missionary preachers who had 'gone out' from the believing community into the world and whose message would draw others away from the community of truth and thus from the truth itself. By affirming them in the truth and exhorting them to continue in genuine love, the elder is thus seeking to protect his readers in advance against the false and destructive influence of these secessionist teachers.

Listening to the text

Context and structure

The formal introduction having been completed, the elder now turns to exhortation. As may be expected in a paragraph designed to motivate his readers to action, he begins with a statement of affirmation expressing his 'great joy' (v. 4) that they have remained faithful to the truth. This reference to 'the truth' links verses 4-6 closely to the introductory paragraph where, although both love and the truth were mentioned, the emphasis was on 'the truth'.

The elder's affirmation of his readers as those who do indeed walk in the truth is followed by an assurance that what the elder is about to ask of his readers is not something new but rather something which arises out of foundational teaching. Twice in the paragraph reference is made to that which was heard 'from the beginning' (vv. 5,6). As we shall see, this assurance is of key importance given the new teaching of the secessionists. Having given this assurance, the elder at last makes the appeal that is the primary focus of the paragraph. His appeal is that both he and his readers must continue to 'love one another' (v. 5). And, lest his readers be in doubt about what such love means in practice, the elder defines love as 'walking according to His (i.e. the Father's) commands' (v. 6), thus underlining the link not only between truth and love but also between love and obedience to the Father.

Although verses 7-11 also constitute part of the main body of the letter, following logically from what is said in verses 4-6, (note the word 'because' with which verse 7 begins), it is preferable for our purposes to treat them as a separate sub-section which, as we saw above, provides the particular context within which the affirmation and exhortation found in verses 4-6 must be understood.

Working through the text

The elder begins by expressing his delight that, in the main, his readers have indeed remained faithful to the truth of the gospel. That the phrase 'great joy' (*lit* rejoiced greatly) is not merely a rhetorical device is clear when we bear in mind the concern that the elder has for his readers. As he has already stated, he loves them in the truth in a relationship which exists 'because of the truth'. And, as we shall see, he is also deeply concerned lest they be turned away from the truth and thus 'lose what they have worked for' (v. 8). Thus, his great joy at finding them 'walking in the truth' is true joy. Furthermore, although the tense of the verb 'to give' is aorist, its syntactical function is durative so that we should understand the writer's 'joy' both as joy experienced at his first encounter with the 'children' and as joy which continues at the time of writing.

Nor should we view the word 'some' in a negative light, as if only a few within the community to which the letter was sent had continued in the truth and the majority had turned away. Though the elder is concerned for his readers, there is no suggestion in the letter that he has been faced with wholesale apostasy. The 'us' of verse 2 is inclusive showing that the truth continued to live both within the elder and his own community as well as within the community of which the readers were a part. This is also consistent with the elder's description of them as 'chosen by God' (v. 1). In fact the word 'some' points us in an altogether different direction. Having himself encountered 'some' from the readers' community and having found that they continue to walk in the truth, the elder has good hopes that the 'some' are evidence of the fact that the 'many' with whom he has not had direct contact also continue to walk in the truth. This again takes us back to the elder's expression of 'great joy'.

As we have already noted, the reason for the elder's joy is that the believers to whom he writes are 'walking in the truth'. Having believed the truth which came to them at the beginning, they have remained faithful to that truth and are seeking to live in the light of it. Nor is this ongoing commitment to the truth merely a matter of loyalty to the elder or to the tradition which he represents, for the call to walk in the truth is in fact a command of the Father (v. 4). As such the privilege and responsibility of walking in the truth belongs to every believer, the elder included, (note the 'us' in verse 2). The elder thus seeks to affirm his readers for their faithfulness to the truth and in so doing to encourage them to continue 'walking in the truth'.

At the same time, the elder reminds his readers that this commitment to walking in the truth is but one part of what the Father commanded. Having commended his readers for walking in the truth, he now urges them also to obey the Father's command which he and they have had 'from the beginning', namely the command to 'love one another' (v. 5). At this point it is important to note the inclusive language that the elder uses. The command of the Father is 'that we love one another'. Although the elder is concerned that his readers should love one another within their own community, he is particularly concerned that the relationship of love between himself as the elder and the community, to whom he is writing, is not undermined by the coming of those who have gone out into the world with a message which was different from that preached from the beginning. In this context, the call to love one another is thus a call to remain in fellowship with the elder and with the community of the truth, the very thing the secessionists have not done.

This understanding of the elder's appeal to his readers enables us to make better sense of the rather difficult verse 6. The verse begins with a definition of what the elder means by love, for he states 'this is love: that we walk in accordance to His commands'. But what does he mean by love? Love for the Father which would fit in with the reference to obedience? Or love for the brothers which is certainly the focus of verse 5 to which verse 6 is connected by the word 'and' at the beginning of the verse? And which commands does the elder have in mind? In the light of verse 4 he would surely include the Father's command to his people that they must continue to walk in the truth, but the plural commands imply more. And this something more is surely the command of verse 5 that the readers and the elder should continue to love one another. Understood in this way, verse 6 thus defines 'love' as ongoing obedience to the Father's twin command to walk not only in truth but also in love. This suggests a broad rather than a narrow understanding of the word 'love' in verse 6 as was in fact the case in verse 3. The love to which the elder refers is love for the Father which manifests in obedience to the Father's twin command and thus also includes love for the brothers.

In the light of this reading, we can thus interpret the word 'it' in the final clause of verse 6 as a reference to the command of the Father rather than a reference to love. The elder thus ends with the statement: 'This (i.e. the twin commands to walk both in truth and in love) is the command (of the Father), just as we heard it from the beginning, so that we may walk in (i.e. obey) it'. The purpose behind the Father's commands is that His people may do them, and it is for this reason that the elder urges His readers to keep not just one but both of the Father's commands.

What then is the love in which the elder urges his readers to walk? It is a discerning love as well as a practical love; a love which though directed to others is also shaped by the truth. It is in fact love which mirrors the love which the Father Himself has made known in Jesus Christ. It is not mere sentiment, but a walk in obedience to and in fellowship with the Father and the Son and in fellowship with others who likewise seek to walk both in love and in truth.

From text to message

Whereas the emphasis of the opening paragraph was on the truth which was closely related to love, the emphasis of verses 4-6 is upon love which is closely related to truth. The elder is thus seeking to protect his readers both from a sentimental love which lacks discernment and from a doctrinaire disengaged view of life within the Christian community. Although the word 'balance' can easily be misapplied in debates about spirituality, the truth is that God's people should be characterised by a true and godly balance, a balance which affirms both truth and love. Sadly this balance is sorely lacking among believers today, a fact which makes the teaching of verses 4-6 with their emphasis on discerning love just as important as the teaching of verses 1-3 with their emphasis on truth.

Getting the message clear: the theme

- While it is important for believers to walk in the truth it is just as important that believers should also walk in love.
- This love will, however, never be expressed without reference to truth and will always find its true expression in fellowship with those who hold the truth.

Getting the message clear: the aim

To encourage believers not only to walk in truth but also to walk in love thus obeying what the Father has commanded from the beginning.

A way in

One way in might be to speak about the issue of balance in the Christian life. Balance may well be a misused concept but it remains a very important one. In the first talk based on verses 1-3, the focus was on the importance of truth, while not neglecting the importance of love. In the second talk based on verses 4-6, the emphasis is upon love, while not neglecting the importance of truth. Those who seek to be followers of the Lord must ensure that they walk in both truth and love and thus maintain a Biblical balance.

Ideas for application

- Every believer should be committed to walking in the truth.
- We should take real joy when we see people persevering in the truth and do everything in our power to encourage them to continue doing so.

- From the very beginning the message of the gospel has always emphasised the importance of both truth and love.
- It is of the utmost importance that believers also walk in love.
- Both truth and love matter equally within the Christian community and we should do all that we can to promote both of these.
- God expects those who claim to love Him to keep His commands and He commands that believers should be people of both truth and love.

Suggestions for preaching

Sermon

People of Truth and Love (2 John 4-6)

1. Introduction
    - The problem with balance
    - The importance of balance
2. A joyful commendation
    - A people walking in the truth
3. An urgent appeal
    - A people called to walk in love
4. An obedient people
    - A people of truth and love

Suggestions for teaching

Questions to help understand the passage

1. How does the elder describe the joy that he feels?
2. What was the cause of his joy?
3. What does the elder mean when he refers to an 'old commandment'?
4. What is the beginning to which the elder refers?
5. What does the phrase the 'commands of God' refer to in this passage?
6. What does the elder urge his readers to do?
7. What is love according to this passage?

Questions to help apply the passage

1. In what way does this passage encourage believers to keep walking in the truth?
2. Why does it matter that believers do indeed remain people of the truth?
3. According to this passage, what commands has God given to us to obey?
4. Why is it hard to maintain the balance between love and truth?
5. What encouragement does this passage give to believers to continue to walk in both truth and love?
6. In what ways is the fellowship between believers destroyed when truth and love are not kept in balance?
7. In what ways has this passage encouraged or rebuked you?

3

Opposing the Trouble Makers (2 John 7-11)

Introduction

Having affirmed his readers in their commitment to walking in the truth and exhorted them to continue walking in love, the elder now warns his readers of the threat posed to their faith by a group of teachers who have 'gone out into the world' (v. 7). The phrase 'gone out' is significant for it underlines the fact that these missionary teachers are in reality secessionists, people who have broken fellowship with the elder and his community. And lest the readers think that the root of this breakaway is a mere difference of opinion over minor things or a personality clash, the elder states that the secessionists have also broken with orthodox belief and are in fact 'antichrists' (v. 7). Thus the work which they do and for which they are seeking support is not Christ's work but wicked work (v. 11), work in which no true believer should or indeed could share.

The elder thus has a twin purpose in 2 John 7-11. First he wants to protect the readers from being led astray themselves by the false teaching of the secessionists (vv. 8,9). Second, he wants to ensure that the teaching of these secessionists does not gain traction and spread to the wider community and so he urges his readers not to provide hospitality or support to them (vv. 10,11).

Listening to the text

Context and structure

As we saw above, there is a close logical connection between verses 4-6 and verses 7-11. Verse 7 begins simply with the words 'because many deceivers...have gone out into the world.' Thus in verses 7-11 the elder provides the context within which his affirmation and exhortation should be read and the reason why they should be taken to heart. The community faced a real threat and it was precisely to safeguard the community that the elder wrote.

Having given the reason for his affirmation and exhortation, the elder next sets out to identify the precise nature of the error that he is warning against, describing the secessionists both as deceivers and as antichrists (v. 7). This identification is important because of the subtle and deceptive nature of the teaching which these missionaries promote. Identification is followed by a stern warning (v. 8) and a clear reminder of both the truth and also of the reward that those who hold firm to the truth will and already do enjoy (v. 9). The paragraph then ends with a further warning, this time against a misguided generosity which makes those who give support to these missionary teachers unwitting sharers in their wicked work (vv. 10-11)!

The warnings having been delivered, the elder concludes his letter with an expression of his desire to visit his readers in the near future and with the customary greetings from their fellow believers (vv. 12-13). We will focus on this closing paragraph in the next section.

Working through the text

Throughout our previous discussion, we noted that the context in which the elder wrote the letter which we know as 2 John, was the very real threat which was posed to the spiritual well-being of the believers among whom the elder and his associates had laboured in the Name of Christ. It is this threat in particular which is now in the forefront of the elder's mind as he writes to warn his readers against the influence of the 'many deceivers' who have 'gone out into the world' (v. 7). Such going out does, of course, speak of zeal and sincerity, but in the context of the letters of John, it also speaks of departure from the community of the faithful and a break with the truth itself. That this is in the elder's mind can be seen from the strong language that he uses to describe these missionary teachers, for in relation both to the truth and the community these men should be seen as 'deceivers' and 'antichrists' (v. 7).

Later on in the passage, the elder will allude to this false teaching as something which purports to be 'progressive' (note his use of the words 'runs ahead' in v. 9), a claim which doubtless made the new teaching so appealing and thus deceptive. Right at the outset, however, the elder states in plain terms what the doctrinal error that lay at the heart of this false teaching is. The hallmark of these missionary teachers was that they did not 'acknowledge Jesus Christ as coming in the flesh' (v. 7). Notwithstanding the present tense of the verb 'to come', what the elder is referring to is a refusal to acknowledge that in the 'flesh', that is in the human person of Jesus, the Christ of God, the Father's Son

(v. 3) had indeed come into the world. Although the elder does not elaborate on the content of this false teaching, it is fair to assume that the phrase 'Jesus Christ as coming in the flesh' was shorthand both for the historical reality and the implications of such a coming and that the readers of the letter knew precisely what the elder had in mind when he spoke in these terms. In 1 John, both the doctrine of the incarnation and the atonement were at stake and there is no reason to doubt that the same is true in 2 John. This is certainly implied by the elder's declaration that believers experience 'grace, mercy and peace' both from the Father and from His Son, Jesus Christ and thus only as a result of the coming in the flesh of Jesus Christ. What was it about the coming of Jesus the Christ in the flesh which made such an experience of the grace of God, the mercy of God and peace with God possible? Surely it was the fact that Jesus the Christ who came in the flesh did so in order to make atonement for the sins that cut people off from this grace, mercy and peace.

And the fact that the elder had the incarnation and atonement in mind is surely also implied by his reference to 'the teaching of Christ' in verse 9. In this context it is best to understand this phrase as a reference to orthodox teaching about Christ, teaching that had been delivered to the readers either by the elder himself or by his associates. The key point about this teaching was that it consisted of a fixed body of truth about Christ, what the elder elsewhere calls 'the truth'. And this truth had not been invented by the elder nor could it be modified by 'anyone' (note the elder's use of the word in verses 9 and 11) – it was truth that both he and they had 'from the beginning' (vv. 5,6). It was this teaching about Jesus the Christ which brought a true experience of God's grace, mercy and peace into the lives of the believers and which made fellowship with both the Father and the Son a reality, for 'whoever continues in the teaching has both the Father and the Son' (v. 9). And it is precisely this authentic fellowship with God that the elder wanted his readers to hold onto and not to lose (v. 8). He thus urges them to 'watch out' (v. 8), to resist the teaching of the 'many deceivers' and 'antichrists' and to hold firm to the teaching which they have received. The word 'continues' in verse 9 is key and stands as the counter to 'runs ahead', an attitude to the teaching which though seemingly 'progressive' is in fact destructive, causing those who follow this path to suffer ultimate loss, the loss of God Himself. The warning could hardly be clearer: 'Anyone who runs ahead and who does not continue in the teaching of Christ does not have God' (v. 9).

In the first section of the paragraph the elder thus reminds his readers about the teaching which brought them spiritual life and which holds out a 'full reward' (v. 8) for them, if they continue to walk faithfully in the truth. The reference to such a 'full reward' is striking and should in all likelihood be understood in contradistinction to what the secessionists were teaching. Were they offering a full experience of God apart from Jesus the Christ, a reward to those who were willing to leave behind the old teaching and 'run ahead' to the new? And was the enjoyment of that 'reward' also contingent on the hearers taking a share in the work of these new teachers by offering them hospitality and support? Such questions cannot be answered with certainty but the scenario which they sketch is not entirely unreasonable, given the elder's insistence on the need to 'continue' rather than 'run ahead' and his appeal for his readers to hold onto what both he and they have 'worked for' (v. 8). Rather than the easy path offered by the new teaching, the elder calls upon his readers to remain loyal to the teaching of Christ and to persevere to the end in their commitment to truth and love as commanded by the Father and as modelled by the Father's Son Jesus Christ.

One thing that is absolutely clear, however, and a point that the elder seeks to underline for his readers in the final section of the passage, is that no one who has the Father and the Son should share in the 'wicked work' in which these deceivers or antichrists were engaged (v. 11). This is, of course, not an assessment that the missionary teachers would have accepted but it is the one which the elder, speaking from the point of view of the truth, feels compelled to give. The word 'wicked' is a striking one and suggests someone or something that is cut off or loosed from God. When we bear in mind that the outcome of the work done by these teachers is that people move away from Jesus the Son and as a consequence are cut off from God the Father, the word seems in fact to be entirely appropriate and the elder's assessment of such work completely correct.

It is because of this assessment of the work of these teachers that the elder not only warns his readers against being led astray by the teaching of the secessionists but also forbids them from offering such teachers any kind of support. The deceivers and antichrists were to receive no hospitality or 'welcome' from the believing community (vv. 10,11). And again the criterion by which such decisions are to be made is not based on the whim of the elder or the community but upon whether those who arrive and who seek such a welcome are true to 'the teaching' of Christ or not. As we shall see in 3 John, if they are true to the teaching of Christ and have gone out for the sake of 'the Name', i.e. the name of Jesus, they are to be welcomed and cared for by all who love the truth. If not, they are to be turned away so that their 'wicked work' may not flourish but rather come to nothing.

From text to message

There are at least two aspects of the elder's teaching in 2 John 7-11 which many people will no doubt find to be unacceptable by today's standards. First, there is the elder's strong description of the rival teachers as deceivers and antichrists. Surely, people will say, such a description of those with whom we may differ theologically is harsh and in fact itself 'un-Christian'! That we differ is unavoidable given our diverse culture and beliefs. That such differences should be cast in such negative terms is intolerable and worthy of censure! Second, others may take issue with the elder's insistence that authentic Christianity is essentially conservative and non-progressive. Surely the church has learnt much over the past centuries and there should therefore be room for theological progress and the development of newer, more modern beliefs. Surely, given the progress we have made, any insistence on the 'old, old story' as the only authentically Christian story is arrogant and thus to be rejected.

Such attitudes are sadly all too familiar, sometimes even among those who ought to know better. And yet, as 2 John 7-11 makes clear, they are not new nor should they be countenanced today any more than they were when the elder wrote. And the reason is not hard to find, for the authentic faith of the Church, the faith that truly saves, is the faith that is loyal to the 'teaching of Christ' as it was first received and then passed on to subsequent generations. We are inheritors not inventors of a message and given what is at stake, namely the true knowledge of God, we will do well not only to hold on to what is true but oppose all that is false, even if we find ourselves out of step with those who prefer a more tolerant way.

Getting the message clear: the theme

Because the Father can only be known through Jesus Christ the Son:–

- Believers are to hold fast to the apostolic teaching about Christ, i.e. the truth about the incarnation and atoning death of Jesus the Christ, the Son of God as the only way to God.

- Believers are in no way to countenance or support teaching which refuses to acknowledge Jesus Christ, his incarnation and atoning death as the only way.

Getting the message clear: the aim

To encourage believers to hold fast to the truth about Jesus Christ as the only way to God and to oppose all teaching that refuses to acknowledge Jesus the Christ, his incarnation and atoning death.

A way in

One way in would be to speak about our current context, especially the intolerance that people feel when it comes to evangelical Christians insisting that Christ is indeed the only way to God. From such an evangelical point of view it is impossible to merely affirm what is true. Given the fact that there is so much false teaching around we also need to expose that which is false. That is exactly what 2 John 7-11 both enables and encourages us to do.

Another way in would be to speak about the Christian faith in terms of a commitment to 'the truth' as something which we have received rather than something which we have the right to change or to reinvent in keeping with current beliefs and fashions. As believers in Christ we are indeed committed to holding fast to the old, old story of Jesus and his love. Stewardship of this same gospel is essential for the spiritual well-being not only of our own generation but also of the generations which follow.

Ideas for application

- The false teacher is a familiar figure in the world today.
- Zeal and sincerity are no guarantee of truth. What is preached must be evaluated before it is accepted.
- The gospel of Jesus the Christ, the Son of God is the only true measure and all teaching must be evaluated against this standard.
- Christians are to take responsibility for what they believe.
- Although Christians are to progress in understanding and to grow in grace, we are never to move on from the truth of the gospel to 'new' truths. In this sense every true believer is to be a conservative.
- Believers are to be discerning about what ministry endeavours they support and should never support anything which is not consistent with the apostolic gospel about Jesus Christ.

Suggestions for preaching

Sermon

True Truth (2 John 7-11)

1. Introduction
    - A world in which everything goes
    - A world full of false teachers
2. Holding fast to the truth
    - The teaching – Jesus Christ in the flesh
    - The call – hold fast to what you have
    - The warning – don't run ahead
    - The promise – a full reward
3. Opposing the error
    - Deceivers and antichrists
    - The only way to the Father
    - Don't buy or sell the lie!
4. Conclusion
    - Work for what is good

Suggestions for teaching

Questions to help understand the passage

1. How does this passage connect with what has gone before?
2. What characterised the teaching of those whom the elder calls deceivers and antichrists?

3. What urgent warning does the elder give to his readers?

4. What does he mean by 'what we have worked for'?

5. What does the elder mean by 'the teaching of Christ'?

6. What do the words 'continue' and 'runs ahead' suggest about the kind of error that the elder was seeking to oppose?

7. What does this passage teach us about the way to fellowship with God?

8. What does this passage teach about the way in which false teaching should be treated?

Questions to help apply the passage

1. Are deceivers and antichrists still present in the world today?

2. In what way do people reject Jesus Christ as coming in the flesh today?

3. How can believers ensure that they do not lose what they have worked for?

4. From this passage, what is the full reward that God promises to those who continue in the teaching of Christ?

5. What does this passage teach about spiritual discernment? How can we grow in this?

6. Why should Christians speak out against false teaching?

7. What standard should we apply when asked to support someone's ministry?

8. How can Christians work against the influence of false teachers?

4
Joyful Fellowship (2 John 12-13)

Introduction

At first glance this final passage of 2 John appears to be nothing more than a traditional letter ending but there is in fact more to it than meets the eye. In particular, the passage reflects the depth of the elder's relationship with his readers, a relationship which as we have already seen exists because of the truth and in the truth. Far from the idea that Christian truth is sterile or divisive, this passage reminds us that the truth of the gospel creates real and lasting fellowship not only with God but also between believers. It is a sense of this gospel fellowship which moves the elder to write as he does, expressing genuine longing to see fellow believers and to be able to share the joy of the Christian fellowship with them. As such the passage reminds us that it is a rare and wonderful privilege to be one of God's true people.

Listening to the text

Context and structure

In 2 John 12, we move from the main body of the letter to the elder's concluding comments. These include: (1)

a reference to the letter itself as an important but not exhaustive statement of all that the elder wishes to say to his readers; (2) a reference to the elder's deep desire to visit his readers in person and by so doing to enter into personal and joyful fellowship with them in a way that communication by letter does not make possible; (3) the passing on of greetings from the community of which the elder is a part. In formal terms, therefore, the material is what would be expected in a concluding paragraph. However, as we noted with the introduction and will see below, even here there are some key distinctives which tie the letter in with its setting and serve to reinforce what the elder has written.

Working through the text

Despite that typical nature of this conclusion there are a number of key things to note. First, we note that the phrase 'I have much to write to you' (v. 12) suggests that although the elder has been at pains to call his readers back to the foundational truth and away from novelty, this does not mean that there is not more that can be said about the authentic Christian life than is contained in his letter. Doubtless, part of the argument of the secessionists would have been that the 'from the beginning' truth as proclaimed by the elder had run its course and that something more was needed. The elder concurs that there is always room for growth and more to say, but he only makes this statement having established quite clearly that this something more does not run ahead from the foundational teaching of Christ. His readers are thus reminded that they are to grow in depth in the truth not away from it.

Second, we note that unlike the secessionists the elder longs to come to the community as one desiring 'face to face' fellowship. Though he is the elder and thus their teacher, and though he is quite willing to exercise spiritual authority over them, the elder at no point sets himself above his readers. The words that the elder uses to describe his desired visit imply shared fellowship in a mutual conversation around the truth. It is a visit centred both around 'talk', i.e. speaking the truth to one another 'face to face' (*lit* mouth to mouth) (v. 12) and mutual joy. And as we have already seen in verse 4 this mutual joy is in and because of the truth. Thus the elder wants both to encourage his readers by his presence and words and be encouraged in their presence and by their words. And here we once again get the hint that the elder has authentic growth and progress rather than the spurious growth and progress offered by the false teachers in view. He thus speaks of 'joy being made complete' by which he means a real but growing joy experienced through familiar truth shared and more deeply understood. What the elder thus envisages is the expression of truth and love at work in the community of believers, that is, authentic Christian fellowship.

Third, we note that the elder sends not only his own personal greetings but the greetings of the community of which he is himself a part. Unlike the secessionists he remains part of the true community of faith and his coming to them is not a 'going out' but in fact a 'coming in' to visit. Nor does he set the community of which he is a part above the community of his readers. They are nothing more or anything less than a 'sister congregation', 'children chosen by God' (vv. 13) and thus recipients of the same grace, mercy and peace from God the Father and from the Lord Jesus Christ that all Christians everywhere enjoy in the fellowship of truth and love.

From text to message

Preaching on a brief concluding paragraph such as 2 John 12-13 may at first seem rather odd and the temptation with this and similar paragraphs is to simply ignore them or to briefly touch on them as part of something larger and more substantial. But careful attention to them in their context very often yields real fruit for teaching and application. Thus these concluding verses of 2 John give us a real opportunity to speak about the value of personal relationships with other believers and of the importance of a humble and fervent desire to experience mutual growth in both truth and love. As we noted above, the fellowship of true believers is a precious reality, one which it is our duty and joy not only to protect but also to promote.

Getting the message clear: the theme

True believers are called to grow in joyful fellowship with other believers within the community of truth and love.

Getting the message clear: the aim

To encourage humble and joyful fellowship between believers.

A way in

One way in would be to talk about the scourge of elitism, especially where it manifests itself among Christian believers. All true believers are chosen by God and experience the grace, mercy and peace that come from God the Father and from His Son Jesus Christ. Yet how easy it is for us to draw lines and distinctions among the people of God; and how easy it is for us to rejoice only in our own particular group rather than in all who belong to the Lord. In this passage the elder models a true and humble commitment to his fellow believers, one which seeks not only to give but also humbly to receive encouragement in the truth that is the birthright of every Christian.

Ideas for application

- Fellowship in the truth is a wonderful and rare privilege.
- Authentic fellowship can only happen around the truth spoken.
- Authentic Christian experience does not exclude spiritual growth.
- All true spiritual growth involves growth in the truth not growth 'beyond' the truth.
- Relationships should matter to believers.
- All believers in the Lord Jesus are equal in the sight of God and members of His one true family.

Suggestions for preaching

Sermon

Face to Face (2 John 12-13)

1. Introduction
    - Us and them *or* why we are better than they are!
2. Face to face
    - Truth shared so that we can grow
    - The joy of truth shared

3. Brothers and sisters in Christ
    - The privilege of all believers
    - The joy of belonging

Suggestions for teaching

Questions to help understand the passage

1. In what way does the phrase 'I have much to write to you' in verse 12 affirm what the elder has already written?
2. What does this phrase suggest about further growth?
3. Why did the elder want to visit his readers personally?
4. What would such a visit involve?
5. What does the phrase 'face to face' (*lit* mouth to mouth) say about the importance of truth for Christian fellowship?
6. How does the elder describe his own community
    - With respect to God?
    - With respect to the community of the readers?

Questions to help apply the passage

1. In what way are the elder's words 'more to write to you' a challenge?
2. In what way are these words an encouragement?
3. What can we learn from the elder's way of addressing his readers?

4. What can we learn from the elder's desire to spend time in person with the readers of his letter?

5. What is the key to authentic and meaningful fellowship among Christians?

6. Why does Christian fellowship matter?

7. How does God view every true believer? How should this affect the way we think about and act toward our fellow Christians?

5
IN TRUTH AND LOVE (2 JOHN 1-13)

Introduction

In our discussion of 2 John, we noted four key truths. First, we noted that the relationship between the elder and the congregation to which he wrote was deep and personal – a true Christian fellowship. Second, we noted that this joyful fellowship existed only because of a common commitment to the truth about Jesus Christ – it was a relationship of 'love in the truth' (v. 1). Third, we noted that this mutual commitment to both truth and love led to a proper concern that Christians should walk in both truth and love, and that the truth, the whole truth and nothing but the truth be proclaimed in the world. Fourth, we noted that the truth that mattered so much to the elder was not abstract truth, but truth about Jesus, the Christ, the Son of God. For the truth to be preached and lived in love thus meant (and means) that Jesus, and Jesus alone, must be at the very centre. Each of these truths are worth exploring and preaching in their own right, and I have attempted to do that in the exegesis and teaching outlines given above. In what follows, I have provided a suggested outline for a single talk on 2 John as a whole, not to encourage us to rush over this rich text, but rather to assist us to keep our eye on the main thing.

Getting the message clear: the theme

- Because truth and love are found in Christ, those who belong to Christ will walk in both truth and love and proclaim the truth in love.
- Because truth and love are inseparable, true believers will not countenance or support anything that is contrary to the truth.

Getting the message clear: the aim

- To encourage believers to walk in truth and love.
- To encourage believers to be discerning about what they do and don't support in the name of Christian mission.

A way in

One way in is to underline the importance of discernment in a world where everything goes. To 'test the spirits' to see if they are from God is both wise and right. But such discernment, if it is to be truly Christian, must be governed by the truth about Jesus. Only in Jesus do we find the perfect combination of truth and love and thus only by remaining focussed on him can our walk and work truly be said to be of God.

Ideas for application

- Love and truth are essential and inseparable in the life of the true believer.

- Those who love God in truth will submit to His rule in their lives.
- Those who love God in truth will acknowledge and proclaim Jesus as the Christ.
- Those who love God in truth will reject and oppose any teaching which does not glorify Jesus as the Christ, the Son of God.

Suggestions for preaching

Sermon

In Truth and Love (2 John 1-13)

1. Introduction
    - What is truth? – a fashionable question
    - Discernment! – a necessary virtue
2. The Fellowship of love and truth (2 John 1-3)
    - Love in the truth
    - Love because of the truth
3. The life of truth and love (2 John 4-6)
    - Keep walking in truth
    - Keep walking in love
    - Truth, love and obedience
4. Standing for truth and love (2 John 7-13)
    - Many deceivers
    - Don't buy the lie

- Don't share in wicked work
- Keep the fellowship of truth and love

Suggestions for teaching

Questions to help understand the passage
(See the teaching questions in the detailed discussion above)

Questions to help apply the passage
(See the application questions in the detailed discussion above)

Part 4
Teaching 3 John

I
True Gospel Friendship (3 John 1)

Introduction

There is something particularly striking about the way in which 3 John begins, something which attracts the reader's attention and gives one pause for thought. The opening words do, of course, reflect the standard epistolary form of address, in this case from the elder to Gaius who is then further described as a 'dear friend in the truth' (KJV). But the sheer brevity of the opening form of address, the lack of the standard words of greeting, the repetition of the word 'love' (twice within the space of ten words), the emphatic use of the personal pronoun 'I' (already present in the verb and thus redundant in terms of mere grammar) and the emphatic placement of the word 'truth' (the final word in the sentence) all suggest that there is more to this single sentence than meets the eye. In particular, the opening words of address of 3 John bring us face to face with what we may call 'true Gospel friendship', a friendship which, as we shall see below, operated in a wonderful way in the service of the gospel and which is thus worth emulating in our own day.

Listening to the text

Context and structure

Given the brevity of the passage, there is not much to say by way of structural or grammatical analysis. The passage certainly identifies the literary genre of 3 John as a personal letter, written for a particular purpose which will become clear as the content of the letter unfolds. Certainly the repetition of the word 'love' and the reference to 'truth' suggest that once again the purpose of the letter, personal though it is, has to do with the promotion of the truth and the expression of love in conjunction with truth. The emphatic use of the personal pronoun 'I' suggests that the relationship that exists between the sender and the recipient is of fundamental importance for the desired goal of the letter to be accomplished. Indeed, as we will see, this relationship is not to be thought of in isolation but in conjunction with other relationships which likewise arise out of a common commitment to love and truth or to be more precise, 'love in truth'.

Commentators are divided about the structure of 3 John and many include verse 2 as part of the introductory greeting, especially in the light of the benediction 'Beloved, I pray (or trust) that all may go well with you...' with which the verse begins. Within 3 John, however, the vocative 'Beloved' (v. 2 KJV) (*cf* vv. 5,11) marks the beginning of a new section, so it is preferable to see verse 1 as the introduction and verses 2-12 as the main body of the letter (see further below).

Working through the text

The opening verse of 3 John identifies the author of the letter simply as 'the elder', a title which, as we saw in our discussion of 2 John 1 (see above), speaks both of relationship and authority. In relational terms the elder refers to Gaius as 'dear friend' (*lit* the beloved one), that is someone whom the elder knows personally and holds in deep affection. Although the title 'the beloved one' could refer to Gaius' relationship with the Lord, it is in this context more likely a reference to the elder's relationship with Gaius, a relationship which the elder values greatly. Gaius is not simply *a* beloved one, but *the* beloved one, a form of address which underlines the value that the elder places on his relationship with Gaius. This fact is further emphasised by the emphatic use of the pronoun 'I' in the final part of the sentence. In order to capture the feel of this opening address we could thus translate 'the elder to Gaius, the beloved one, whom I, even I, love in the truth.' In a context in which Diotrephes is using his authority to speak against the elder and to oppose the missionary preachers who have come from the elder's community (cf vv. 9-10), the elder wants to secure his relationship with those who are his children in the Lord (cf v. 4), so that they may continue to work together for the truth (cf v. 8). And to this end the relationship between the elder and Gaius was clearly of fundamental importance.

Notwithstanding the affectionate nature of the elder's relationship with Gaius, the elder is also concerned to exercise true spiritual authority. As in 2 John 1, the clause is literally 'whom I love in truth', but the use of the definite article in verses 3 and 4 make it likely that the article should be assumed in verse 1 as well, as was the case at the beginning of 2 John. The elder's relationship with Gaius and with his other children is 'in the truth' (v. 1, cf v. 4) and it is thus 'the truth' that must hold ultimate sway not only over the elder but over Gaius as well. By referring to himself as the elder, he thus also reminds Gaius of his authority and his role to commend those who walk in the truth (e.g. Gaius) and to oppose those who stand against the truth, no matter what status they may hold or claim for themselves (e.g. Diotrephes).

Although the elder does not clarify what is meant by 'the truth', it is clear from verse 7 that the truth is closely linked with 'the Name', so that we may assume that here as elsewhere in the Johannine epistles 'the truth' refers to the truth about Jesus Christ. Thus we may conclude that the opening verse of 3 John serves to recall and to stir up gospel friendship, not merely for its own sake, but, as we shall see below, in order to ensure those who belong to the truth may indeed 'work together for the truth', the whole truth and nothing but the truth.

From text to message

Although the introductory comments of 3 John are particular to the relationship between Gaius and the elder, they nevertheless model a commitment to such relationships of 'love in the truth' and thus challenge the reader of the letter to a similar commitment. We thus need not only to ask how the elder begins his letter to Gaius, but why he begins his letter in this way. Authentic though the relationship was in its own terms, it was, as we shall see from the body of the letter, in particular the value of the relationship for the spread of the truth that was in the elder's mind when he wrote. It is this same factor that should thus be in our minds as we teach the passage, encouraging our hearers to cultivate and to maintain true gospel friendships so that the gospel may spread.

Getting the message clear: the theme

Gospel relationships are precious and worth maintaining for the sake of the truth.

Getting the message clear: the aim

To encourage the maintenance and wise use of gospel relationships.

A way in

One way in to the passage could be to speak about how much more effective a message is if it is communicated within the context of meaningful relationships. This is true in general and it is certainly true when it comes to the Christian message. And it is this focus on truth in personal relationship that we find modelled in 2 John 1, a gospel friendship which recognises that such working together for the truth is the key way that the truth will be made known.

Another way in to the passage could be to speak about the value of relationships. God has made us relational beings and thus relationships are very important to us. Although all relationships are precious, there is something particularly wonderful about gospel relationships. They are, of course, precious in their own right for love in the truth is the environment in which we grow as Christians. But gospel relationships are also precious because of the strength they give to gospel endeavour. Where gospel relationships are strong there the gospel will prosper.

Ideas for application

- As Christians we share in gospel relationships, the expression of love in the truth.

- It is right that we love our fellow believers and value our relationships with them.
- Authentic Christian relationships always involve both love and truth.

Suggestions for preaching

Sermon

Gospel Friendship (3 John 1)

1. Introduction
   - Relationships – a precious gift
   - Gospel relationships – a special privilege
2. The shape of Gospel relationships
   - Founded on truth
   - Expressed in love
   - Person to person
3. The promise of Gospel relationships
   - Standing together in love
   - Working together for the truth

Suggestions for teaching

Questions to help understand the passage

1. What title does the author of the letter use to describe himself?
2. What does this title signify?

3. How does the elder describe his relationship with Gaius?
4. What is the significance of the personal pronouns in this verse?
5. In what way does 3 John 1 show that love and truth are inseparable?

Questions to help apply the passage

1. What does this verse teach us about the nature of gospel relationships?
2. What does this verse teach us about the value of gospel relationships?
3. In what way is this verse a challenge or an encouragement to us?

2
Walking together in the Truth (3 John 2-4)

Introduction

Having renewed and re-affirmed his relationship with Gaius in the opening words of the letter, the elder now assures Gaius of his personal interest and especially of the great joy that he takes in the fact that Gaius continued to remain faithful to the truth, despite the pressure that he had experienced from people like Diotrephes. The opening wish or prayer (v. 2) focuses on Gaius' general well-being, and as such it reminds us that no false dichotomy should be created within the disciple's life between physical and spiritual matters. But the reference to Gaius' soul or 'spiritual life' at the end of verse 2 and the expression of the elder's great joy at the news that Gaius had remained faithful to the truth in verses 3-4, make it clear that the main focus of the passage is upon Gaius' spiritual well-being. The purpose of the passage is thus to affirm and strengthen Gaius in his commitment to keep walking in the truth, notwithstanding the opposition he faced.

Listening to the text

Context and structure

In terms of *genre* and rhetorical purpose, 3 John 2-4 is an *exordium,* an introductory literary device whereby the author established rapport with his readers. It was typical of such passages to include good wishes or a prayer for the well-being of the recipients as well as positive statements about the recipient's character and behaviour. This is clearly the pattern that we find in 3 John 2-4.

The word 'beloved' (KJV) at the beginning of verse 2 not only marks the start of a new section (see above), but also echoes the use of the term in verse 1, thus linking the opening address and the exordium. As we shall see, it is in particular the relationship of 'love in the truth', introduced in verse 1 that will be built upon in verses 2-4.

Having reminded Gaius of his personal commitment and genuine interest in Gaius' well-being (v. 2), the elder next affirms Gaius in his faithful commitment to the truth. News had reached the elder that Gaius continued to walk in the truth (v. 3) and the elder's response is to expresses his great joy to Gaius that this is indeed the case (vv. 3,4). As we shall see in our discussion of verses 5-8, this affirmation provides the basis for the elder's appeal to Gaius that he continue to walk in the truth and to love others who likewise walk in the truth by 'welcoming' and supporting them. The fact that verse 5 begins with the vocative 'beloved' (KJV) indicates that verses 5-8 form a new, if closely related, section of the letter.

Working through the text

For the second time in as many verses, we find the words 'dear friend' or 'beloved' used to describe Gaius. As we noted above, the word is the elder's preferred form of address for

Gaius and one that should therefore be noted. Whatever the circumstances that Gaius faced within his own community (and as we shall see below they were certainly difficult), the elder wanted Gaius to know without a shadow of a doubt that he had the elder's personal support and affection. This must certainly have been a great encouragement to Gaius as he sought to stand up for the truth as he had received it from the elder.

The reference to the elder's wish or prayer that in all things, including Gaius' health, things may 'go well' (v. 2) did far more than tick the box of epistolary convention. It showed that the elder had a real and personal concern for Gaius the man, and not simply for Gaius the worker for the truth. As such this expression of genuine interest in Gaius provided an important model not only for those in the church, but also for those in leadership. If, as is likely, 3 John was read within the congregation, the elder's attitude to Gaius would have provided a stark contrast to the attitude and behaviour of Diotrephes whom Gaius at the very least, knew to be self-centred (*cf* v. 9).

But the prayer and the reference to Gaius' general well-being also provided the elder with a vivid backdrop against which to paint a picture of what is of the greatest value in life. Important though Gaius' general well-being was, it was his spiritual health, the health and prosperity of his 'soul' (v. 2) that was the primary focus of the elder's interest and it was the fact that Gaius was 'faithful to the truth' and 'continuing to walk in the truth' (v. 3) that gave the elder his greatest joy (vv. 3,4). Thus in the remainder of the paragraph it is this fact about Gaius that the elder dwells upon.

The news that Gaius was 'faithful to the truth' (*lit* 'in the truth') and continuing to 'walk in the truth' reached the elder through the 'coming' and 'testimony' of 'the brothers' (v. 3). It is not clear who these brothers were, nor is their identity germane to the elder's point. What is clear is that they had witnessed Gaius' faithfulness to the truth first-hand, perhaps through the very kind of 'welcome' that the elder refers to in verse 5, and were thus able to testify to it. And it was this news about Gaius that prompted the elder's 'great joy' (v. 3). Indeed, the elder goes on to say that the joy he felt at receiving this news about Gaius was greater than any other joy that he could have had. The comparative 'no greater joy than' (v. 4) correctly translates the original and once again underlines how much it mattered to the elder that his children continued to walk in the truth. It also provides the context for the elder's later comments reflecting his dismay at the news that Diotrephes who was part of the church did not share his commitment to and joy in the truth. One must assume that the news about Diotrephes and his 'malicious gossip' had also reached the elder through the testimony of the same brothers and that it was this bad news as much as the good news about Gaius that had caused him to describe the greatness of his joy in such exuberant terms.

As we have already noted and will see again in our discussion of verses 5-8, the elder's focus on Gaius' spiritual well-being and his affirmation of Gaius as someone who continues to walk in the truth provided the foundation upon which he could make his appeal to Gaius both to welcome and support those who had gone out for the sake of the Name (v. 7).

From text to message

Two key things are highlighted within 3 John 2-4 and are worth considering as one prepares to teach this passage today. The first of these is, of course, the elder's caring and interested attitude toward Gaius both as a person and as someone who is working for the truth. Within a world in which productivity and results rather than people matter, this authentic relational approach to people is a great encouragement and a wonderful example. It certainly challenges the lie that the church is no different to the world in that it just 'uses' people for its own ends. And it certainly exposes as 'evil' any attitude or action toward people which fails to care about them as persons in their own right.

The second and primary thing that the passage highlights is that it is of fundamental importance that those who represent the truth do indeed remain faithful to the truth and continue to walk in the truth. The elder's joy over the news that this was the case with Gaius reminds us just how important and precious such gospel relationships are. It also reminds us that we must make every effort to affirm those whom we know and who are continuing in the truth, particularly if, like Gaius, they are doing so in the face of opposition and hostility. Feelings of isolation can very easily give rise to doubts about whether such a commitment to the truth is worthwhile, and a word of encouragement and affirmation will certainly go a long way to encouraging others to keep going.

Getting the message clear: the theme

- People are of great importance in authentic gospel relationships

- News that believers are continuing in the truth should give us great joy

Getting the message clear: the aim

To encourage people to be personally committed to one another in gospel relationships

A way in

One way in might be to ask the question about what gives us the most joy in life. There are, of course, many things that we could mention – the joy of family, the joy of success, the joy of deep friendship – but for the believer the deepest joy that is ours is surely spiritual joy, joy in and through the gospel. The New Testament like the Old speaks, of course, of the joy of the Lord, joy which is ours in and through our relationship with Christ. But it also speaks about real joy found in the Lord's work in the lives of others, especially those whom we love or are responsible for. It is this joy that we find described in 3 John 2-4.

Another way in might be to speak about the 'way of the world' as being non-relational, especially when it comes to business, productivity and the bottom line. As believers we are to have a very different viewpoint to that of the world, especially when it comes to the relationships within the Christian community. That very different mentality and approach to people is modelled for us in 3 John 2-4. Although the elder is concerned that Gaius should continue to work in community for the truth, his relationship with Gaius is personal and reflects real integrity. The elder takes a genuine interest in Gaius' welfare and so doing sets an example which we should follow.

Ideas for application

- Relationships within the Christian community should be real and authentic. People are not there simply to be used.

- It is important for us to make progress in our spiritual lives. Our souls are of the utmost importance and should never be neglected in the pursuit of other things.
- Our commitment to the truth should be real and evident to all.
- We should take a real interest in the spiritual well-being of our fellow believers.
- News that our fellow believers are progressing well spiritually should give us real joy.

Suggestions for preaching

Sermon

Gospel joy (3 John 2-4)

1. Introduction
    - Our favourite things
    - The joy of the Lord
2. The elder's prayer
    - Progress in all things
3. The elder's joy
    - News from afar
    - Faithful to the truth
    - Incomparable joy
4. Conclusion
    - Something worth treasuring
    - An example worth following

Suggestions for teaching

Questions to help understand the passage

1. What is the elder's way of addressing Gaius?
2. What does the elder hope and pray for Gaius'? Why does he mention this to Gaius?
3. What gave the elder great joy? What was the occasion of this joy?
4. What made the elder's joy particularly great?
5. What is the focal point of the passage?

Questions to help apply the passage

1. In what way does the elder's prayer model good relationships?
2. What does the passage encourage every believer to do?
3. What does this passage teach about reputation and legacy as a believer?
4. In what way has the passage challenged or encouraged you?
5. What example does the elder set for us?

3
Walking together for the Truth (3 John 5-8)

Introduction

At the heart of this passage we find a simple yet urgent request. In contrast to Diotrephes who 'does what is evil' (v. 11) and 'refuses to welcome other believers' (v. 10), Gaius is urged by the elder to 'do well' (v. 6 KJV) and to continue to welcome and support those who have gone out 'for the Name', that is, to make the name of Jesus known.

In seeking to encourage Gaius in this, the elder gives us three important and relevant reasons why our commitment to the truth of the gospel should also be shown in practical support of true gospel mission. First, such support is of the utmost importance for those who have gone out, for in a world where pagans will give to everything and anything, they will not give to Christian mission. Thus those who go out for the Name are dependent upon those who believe in the Name (v. 7). Second, by supporting such people we have the privilege of working together with them and with the Lord in gospel work (v. 8). Thus we are reminded that it takes partnership in gospel work if we want to see gospel growth. Third, and foundational to the above, there is the fact that in the authentic Christian life, truth and love are inseparable. Gaius who was faithful to the truth was also a man of love for the brothers, even those whom he did not know personally. In this passage the elder reminds us that we would indeed all do well to follow his example.

Listening to the text

Context and structure

As in the previous passage, this new section begins with the vocative 'beloved' (KJV) (v. 5), once again in affirmation of the relationship between the elder and Gaius. This is followed by a description of Gaius' faithfulness and love in action, faithfulness and love that was reported 'to the church' (v. 6) by those who had benefited from it. Logically, this testimony to Gaius' faithfulness ties in with the testimony mentioned in verse 3 and as such is part of the basis of the elder's great joy. Those who have testified are in all likelihood to be identified with those who have gone out for the Name (v. 7), perhaps the self-same people whom Diotrephes refused to welcome. In parallel with this affirmation of Gaius we have the elder's appeal to Gaius to continue to act in this generous fashion (v. 6b), an appeal which the elder not only makes, but which he is willing to own as an obligation for every believer, himself included (v. 8).

The focus then shifts from Gaius and his willing partnership in the gospel as a man of truth and love to Diotrephes, who loves to be first (v. 9). Verses 9-12 thus constitutes a separate paragraph, in which Diotrephes is contrasted not only with Gaius, but also with Demetrius, a man of whom all who belong to the truth, indeed even the truth itself, speak well.

Working through the text

As in verse 2, the elder addresses Gaius as one of his beloved children (cf v. 4 KJV), thus affirming his relationship with Gaius. But in this passage the title 'beloved' (KJV) has additional force, for the elder seeks not only to affirm Gaius in their relationship and in what he has done for the brothers, he also wants to urge him to continue to do so, no matter what opposition he may face. There is no doubt that the reminder of the elder's own commitment to Gaius would have been a strong incentive for Gaius to carry out the elder's request.

Having addressed Gaius in this way, the elder turns his attention to the 'testimony' that he has received concerning what Gaius has done for the brothers. This testimony, made to the church by those who had benefitted from Gaius' 'faithful work' (v. 5), bears witness to the fact that Gaius made every effort in practice (note the use of the words 'are doing' and 'are working ' in verse 5) to serve the brothers, even those who were strangers to him (v. 5). The phrase 'the brothers and the strangers' in the original could be translated either as 'the brothers who are strangers' or as 'the brothers, including those who are strangers'. The latter is preferable since there is no reason to think that every missionary who benefited from Gaius' help was a stranger to him. What is clear is that personal relationship was not the only motivating factor behind Gaius' faithful service. Rather, as we shall see below, it seems that the basis for Gaius' service of these missionary preachers was a common commitment to the truth which they preached. Strikingly, this work and effort on Gaius' part is summed up in a single word, namely, 'love' (v. 6). Gaius, the man known for 'walking in the truth' (v. 3), is also a man known for 'walking in love' (v. 6). Faithful to the truth, Gaius is also attested as a man who is 'faithful' in what he has done for the brothers. Once again, love and truth are seen to be inseparable in the life of the true believer.

The fact that love and truth are inseparable is seen in particular in the fact that Gaius has given welcome and support to those who went out 'for the sake of the Name'. The name referred to is, without doubt, the name of Jesus so that those who went out are to be seen not only as believers in Jesus but missionaries for Jesus. Thus by welcoming and supporting them, Gaius is in fact a fellow worker for the truth (v. 8). Nor should the practical value of his work be underestimated, for the elder reminds Gaius that those who had gone out for the name did not receive any help from the pagans (v. 7). The success of their mission, essential if the Name was to become known, was utterly dependent on the good work of believers like Gaius. Indeed, given that this is the case, the elder adds a final statement obligating all believers to take a similar attitude. Every believer, the elder included (note the inclusive pronoun 'we') 'ought therefore to show hospitality to such people' (v. 8).

The word translated 'hospitality' (NIV) can be rendered more generally as 'give support' (so e.g. ESV). In the ancient world, of course, the intersection of the two meanings would have been quite natural, for no missionary endeavour would have succeeded without the provision of a place to stay or willingness on the part of the hosts to share their meals with such visitors. Occasionally those who were welcomed would be able to contribute, but this was by no means always the case. Indeed, if we look more closely at verse 6 and bearing in mind the happy ambiguity of the word, it seems that the elder is urging Gaius not only to continue providing hospitality and succour to such missionary preachers but also to 'send them on their way in a manner which honours God'. This is almost certainly a reference to some kind of financial support as well, perhaps to help with the costs of a journey or to provide food along the way or perhaps to cover the costs of staying at an inn if no Christian hospitality was forthcoming.

In conclusion then, we note that for all the affirmation of Gaius as a man faithful to the truth and faithful in the love that he had shown to the brothers, the primary objective of the passage was so-called 'praise and blame', intended to increase Gaius' commitment to a set of values and way of behaviour that he had already embraced, but which needed to be strengthened. Indeed, this is not merely the purpose of this particular passage but of the letter as a whole. That such a strengthening of Gaius' resolve and commitment to these things was indeed necessary and thus important will be seen in the next paragraph. In it the focus shifts away from Gaius and his positive example and onto Diotrephes, a man of obvious influence within the church, but whose influence was used not to promote the truth but to spread 'malicious nonsense' (v. 10) about the elder and those who had gone out for the sake of the truth and in the Name of the Lord.

From text to message

As we have just noted, the primary aim of 3 John 5-8 was and is to encourage and strengthen those who are faithful to the truth, to keep working together for the truth and in love to keep on providing support to those whose task it is to make this truth known. In a world as spiritually needy as ours, there could hardly be a more important or more timeous message for the church. And all the more so, given the fact that so many missionary organisations and gospel initiatives seem to be battling for sufficient funds.

What is also particularly fresh and helpful, is the way in which 3 John 5-8 addresses this matter. Unlike so many appeals for support, the passage is entirely free from emotive or manipulative language. The urgency of the matter is clearly in view, as is the personal appeal. But the latter is couched in simple, matter of fact terms, arising from a robust theology and a practical point of view. In short, those who are faithful to the truth and to the Name of Jesus will surely want to see that Name made known. This, indeed, is supremely what honours God. But for this to happen, missionaries must be sent out on behalf of the Name and this can only happen if Christians will commit themselves to working together for the truth and to providing for the financial needs of such missionary preachers. The world, opposed as it is to Jesus, will never give support to such evangelistic endeavours. Therefore it is both the great privilege and the common obligation of all believers to support such gospel work. It is as simple as that!

Getting the message clear: the theme

Because truth and love are inseparable, those who walk in the truth will work together for the truth in supporting gospel work.

Getting the message clear: the aim

To encourage believers in Jesus to support gospel work and to do so more and more.

A way in

One way in could be to speak about the many appeals for help that come across our path every day. As believers in

Christ, and as those who have concern and compassion for our neighbour, we are often moved by such appeals and feel that we ought to help in some way. What is striking, though, and rather disturbing, is that more and more missionary organisations are languishing because of a lack of funding. This must inevitably raise the question: In a world full of deserving causes who will stand behind the cause of the gospel and work to see it grow? John's answer to Gaius in the first century and his answer to us today is simple. If the gospel is to grow then it is we who are to fund its growth. This is our responsibility and our very great privilege.

Ideas for application

- Truth and love are inseparable in the Christian life.
- Those who are faithful to the truth should work together for the truth.
- Believers in Jesus have both the responsibility and the privilege of supporting gospel work.
- Because truth and love are inseparable, believers should be discerning about what and who they support.
- If believers don't support gospel work, no one else will.

Suggestions for preaching

Sermon

Working together for the truth (3 John 5-8)

1. Introduction
    - A world full of needs
    - The greatest need of all

2. The example of Gaius
    - Faithful to the truth
    - Faithful in serving the brothers
    - Discerning but non discriminating
    - A faithful worker for the truth
3. The elder's appeal
    - Keep up the good work
    - The extra mile
4. Conclusion
    - A unique and urgent task
    - A God given-privilege

Suggestions for teaching

Questions to help understand the passage

1. How does the elder address Gaius?
2. Why does he adopt this form of address here?
3. What was true about Gaius?
4. What did this behaviour demonstrate?
5. What was the elder urging Gaius to do?
6. Why was this of such great importance?
7. What attitude ought believers have to the truth?

Questions to help apply the passage

1. What incentives does this passage give us for supporting gospel work?

2. What criteria does this passage give us for supporting gospel work?
3. What lessons does this passage provide for those who are seeking support?
4. What does this passage teach about the importance of gospel partnership?
5. On what basis must such partnerships operate in order to be God honouring?
6. Within a world full of appeals for help, where should giving for the growth of the gospel feature?
7. Should Christians give to causes which pagans would also support?
8. How would you respond to someone who says that this passage forbids Christians from accepting financial assistance from unbelievers?

4
Follow what is Good (3 John 9-12)

Introduction

Although it is never pleasant, opposition in gospel work is not something unexpected in this world. For all its claims about truth, tolerance and love, the world does not tolerate the truth about God and His love for us in Jesus Christ. As Jesus Himself taught: 'light has come into the world but people loved darkness rather than light because their deeds were evil' (John 3:19). So it comes as no surprise that people who reject the light should also reject those who try to point them to Jesus who is the Light. What is distressing, though, is when such opposition to gospel work comes from those who claim to be in the light and who name the Name of Christ. What is difficult to understand and hard to bear is when those who should be walking in the truth and working for the truth end up resisting the truth and opposing others who work for the truth. And that, it would seem, is the situation that Gaius and the elder faced with Diotrephes, the primary subject of 3 John 9-12.

The passage itself, though it speaks about Diotrephes, is not directed to him but to Gaius. Nor was it a case of the elder, in talking about Diotrephes, engaging in the kind of 'malicious gossip' of which the latter was guilty. When the opportunity arose, the elder had every intention of confronting Diotrephes face to face. So we can only assume that it was necessary to address the behaviour of Diotrephes in a letter to Gaius; first, so that Gaius himself would not be swayed from his good work or intimidated by the actions of Diotrephes; and second, so that the church, whom the elder considered to be among his children and to be 'friends' (v. 14), might by hearing what the elder had written about Diotrephes, determine to act and to take their stand with the elder and his interests rather than with those who opposed him.

Listening to the text

Context and structure

Having affirmed and exhorted Gaius regarding his work for the missionary preachers, the elder changes the subject to Diotrephes, a man 'who loves to be first' (v. 9). The change of subject indicates a new section of the letter, one which is nevertheless still closely related to the theme of the letter and to the elder's primary concerns. The paragraph consists of two sub-sections. The first (vv. 9-10) addresses Diotrephes and his self-important behaviour and underlines the elder's total opposition to such behaviour. The second (vv. 11-12) urges Gaius to follow what is good rather than what is evil (i.e. Diotrephes' example) and commends Demetrius to Gaius as a man of truth who, as the bearer of the letter and an ambassador for the Name, is not only to be welcomed but sent on his way in a manner which honours God. This then leads to a final paragraph in which the writer repeats his desire to visit soon and sends greetings to Gaius and to the friends within the community.

Working through the text

Opposing Diotrephes (vv. 9-10)

The first person singular 'I wrote' (v. 9) with which the paragraph begins, refers to a separate communication, but not necessarily to one of which Gaius was unaware. There has been a fair amount of debate about whether Gaius and Diotrephes were part of the same congregation or not and the matter is not easily resolved merely on the internal evidence of the letter itself. The wording 'the church' does suggest a single congregation of which both men were a part. If that was indeed the case, the elder could thus well be saying 'I wrote to the church', (*as you know*), 'but Diotrephes...will not welcome us' (v. 9). This would suggest that the letter to which the elder refers was a letter commending the missionary preachers as men of the truth and thus as worthy of welcome. Since, as he reminds Gaius in connection with Demetrius, 'you know that our testimony is true', the fact that Diotrephes refused to accept the elder's request or welcome his emissaries constituted a serious breach of fellowship, tantamount to a rejection not only of the elder's authority but also of the truth which he represented. Little wonder then that he can refer to Diotrephes' conduct as 'evil' (v. 11).

The reason behind this extraordinary conduct by Diotrephes was the fact that he loved 'to be first' (v. 9). Thus, rather than showing love for the elder or for those who had gone out for the Name, he was a man overcome with love of self. And rather than putting the gospel first, he put himself first. And, as a result of this inordinate love of self, he not only refused to welcome the missionaries himself, but used his position in the church to stop others from doing so, even to the point of having them excommunicated (v. 10). We are not sure what his position in the church was, but it is clear that he exercised a fair amount of authority, though sadly not in the service of the truth but in service of self. Needless to say, Diotrephes would have had his own reasons and ready answers to justify his conduct. The reference to 'malicious rumours' (v. 10) suggests that he had attempted to validate his behaviour by discrediting the elder and those whom the elder had sent out. Either way, his conduct was viewed by the elder in a very serious light, to the point that it raised questions about his relationship with God (see below). And it was for this reason rather than any concern for his own personal dignity, that the elder assured Gaius, and through him the church, that when the elder was able to make his long desired visit, he would 'call attention to what he (*Diotrephes*) is doing' (v. 10). Clearly the elder felt that in the interests of the truth, conduct, such as that of Diotrephes, had to be exposed for what it actually was, rather than what Diotrephes claimed it to be.

Encouraging Gaius (vv. 11-12)

Having thus drawn Gaius' attention to what Diotrephes was in fact doing, the elder once again urges him to imitate what is good and to continue to walk both in the truth and in love toward those whose task it was to promote the truth. The now familiar form of address 'beloved' (KJV) is once again calculated to re-affirm the elder's relationship with Gaius and to add weight to the elder's appeal. Perhaps it had the additional function of countering what Diotrephes had been gossiping about the elder, namely that the absentee elder did not in fact care about the church or the potential harm that could come to it if it welcomed such enthusiastic preachers. Whatever the case, the elder was adamant that Diotrephes' conduct was in fact 'evil (*lit* bad) behaviour' (v. 11) and that it was of the utmost importance that Gaius and the church at large should not imitate it.

Nor was the matter simply to be dismissed as an expression of ecclesiastical party spirit or as a personality clash. The bad behaviour that Diotrephes manifested was in fact typical of a person who 'has not seen God' (v. 11) and therefore does not know God. The good that the elder was anxious for Gaius to imitate was nothing less than conduct appropriate to those who are 'from God' (v. 11). Put differently, as far as the elder was concerned the welcome and support of the missionary preachers who had gone out for the Name was in fact a gospel issue, one in which obedience was of great importance. Hence, the elder's urgent appeal to Gaius to continue to obey as he had in fact previously been doing.

One final question arises and that is to do with the role of Demetrius in the passage. Most of the commentaries view Demetrius as a counterpoint to Diotrephes and thus as someone whose own 'good' conduct Gaius is urged to imitate. But there is no reference in the passage to Demetrius as someone who offered hospitality or support to the visitors. What we do in fact have are multiple commendations of Demetrius' credentials. He is 'well spoken of by everyone', he is well spoken of 'by the truth itself' (i.e. a man faithful to the truth just as Gaius was) and he is well spoken of by the elder and the elder's community, a testimony which Gaius knew could be trusted (v. 12). In my opinion, these credentials therefore point to Demetrius not as a man to be imitated but as a man to be welcomed and supported. In other words, Demetrius served as an example of the integrity of the kind of missionary preachers who had gone out on account of the Name and was thus a classic example of why such people ought to have been welcomed and helped. By refusing to welcome Demetrius, a man spoken well of, not merely by the elder but by everyone, even by the truth itself, Diotrephes showed himself for what he really was, not a man with a love for the truth and the brothers, but a man with a love for himself. By welcoming Demetrius, Gaius was thus shown to be a man of the truth and a man of love, to the honour of God and the great joy of the elder.

From text to message

In preparing to speak on a passage like 3 John 9-12 it is, of course, easy to think of particular individuals, perhaps even church leaders, who have used their position of authority to obstruct true gospel endeavour. Such occurrences are sadly more and more common, particularly, though not exclusively, within the so-called traditional denominations. Given the frustration we feel at such behaviour, it is easy to use a passage like this to 'name and shame' such people.

While it is true that the elder names Diotrephes it should be born in mind that the elder is not taking a cheap shot at him. He has every intention of confronting Diotrephes personally about his conduct. Furthermore, it is clear that the elder's motivation is to encourage Gaius to continue in his support of gospel work and to strengthen the congregation in this regard. There is thus a positive purpose behind the paragraph and it is important that this not be lost from sight when it is being taught. That having been said, the elder is quite clear about the importance of those who have authority, using their privileged position to promote rather than to hinder the gospel and there is certainly no harm done when this point is made in the appropriate manner.

Getting the message clear: the theme

- Those with influence and authority within the church should use their position for the promotion of the gospel.
- It is always wrong to oppose the growth of the gospel.

Getting the message clear: the aim

- To warn against actions that hinder the spread of the gospel.
- To encourage practical support for the spread of the gospel.

A way in

One way in could be to speak about the responsibility that those who are in authority have to act with integrity in their particular field. This is true at all levels of leadership and it is certainly true of those who have authority within the church. When such authority is abused for personal gain or prestige, God is dishonoured and the cause of the gospel suffers. Such a situation seems to have developed within the church to which the elder had written and it was something which the elder could not allow to continue. From what the elder says we are able to glean principles and priorities that will foster rather than hinder gospel growth.

Ideas for application

- Diotrephes' attitude and actions are important warnings against self-centredness, especially when it comes to gospel work.
- When love of self predominates, God's glory and God's work suffers.
- When love of self predominates, love of others will be absent.
- Those who oppose gospel work when they have the opportunity to promote it should be challenged and urged to repent.
- Support of gospel work is one of the evidences of a genuine relationship with God.
- We should do everything in our power to give practical support of gospel work.

Suggestions for preaching

Sermon

For the sake of the gospel (3 John 9-12)

1. Introduction
    - The privilege and responsibility of leadership
2. Opposing Diotrephes
    - A man who should have known better
    - A man who loved himself
    - The destructive fruit of self-centred leadership
        - unwelcomed brothers

    - excluded brothers
    - malicious gossip

3. Encouraging Gaius
    - Imitate what is good
    - Honour God
    - Welcome brothers like Demetrius
4. Conclusion
    - The privilege and responsibility of gospel work
    - Work together for the sake of the gospel

Suggestions for teaching

Questions to help understand the passage

1. When and why did the elder write to the church?
2. How did Diotrephes respond to the elder's letter?
3. Why did he respond in this way?
4. How did Diotrephes' self-centredness manifest itself within the church?
5. What was the 'bad conduct' that Gaius was to eschew? Why?
6. What good behaviour was Gaius to imitate? Why?
7. What do we learn from the passage about Demetrius?
8. How did the elder want Gaius to respond to Demetrius?

Questions to help apply the passage

1. What warning does this passage give to those in leadership?
2. To what end should those with influence within the church use their position?
3. How should we respond when those in leadership act in ways that hinder the spread of the gospel?
4. Of what is opposition to gospel growth a symptom?
5. What should characterise those who know God?
6. In what way has this passage challenged or encouraged you regarding your own support of gospel work?

5
Final Greetings (3 John 13-14)

Introduction

As in 2 John, the elder ends his letter to Gaius with a statement of his intention to visit 'soon' (v. 14) and to rather discuss the matters raised in the letter and any other matters 'face to face' (v. 14). As we noted in our discussion of the end of 2 John, this language is relational and reflects the elder's personal approach to those who are his brothers in the Lord, especially his children in the faith. As we shall see, there are some variations in comparison with the ending of 2 John and it is worth noting these because they do help to cast further light on the situation that the letter was intended to address and correct

Listening to the text

Context and structure

In 3 John 13-14, we move from the main body of the letter to its conclusion. As with its opening words, so the words of final greeting are typical of a first century letter. The elder informs Gaius that there is more to be said than can be said, given the practical constraints of the letter ('pen and ink' (v. 13). He assures Gaius of his desire to visit and his intention to do so 'soon' (v. 14). The addition 'soon' (not in 2 John) is striking and may well suggest that part of the malicious gossip of Diotrephes included the fact that the elder's personal absence showed a lack of love and care for the congregation on his part. The final greetings are typical, though, in a situation where divisions would clearly have existed as a result of Diotrephes' actions, the words 'peace' and 'friends' are striking.

Working through the text

The elder's statement that he has 'much to write' to Gaius is certainly a clear indication that he took a personal interest in Gaius' welfare and that he was not simply using Gaius to further his own cause in the spat with Diotrephes. From the very beginning the elder's relationship with Gaius had been one of 'love in the truth' and that certainly is reflected in his final words. The desire for a 'face to face' conversation with Gaius was thus motivated by this love in the truth. It stands in marked contrast to the other face to face encounter, namely that between the elder and Diotrephes. Such an encounter was designed not to encourage but rather to expose and to rebuke.

As we noted above, the elder mentions specifically that he hopes to visit 'soon'. It is just possible that he stressed this fact in 3 John because of the gossip that Diotrephes had been spreading. The elder wants Gaius to be in no doubt that he values his relationship with Gaius and with the church. Any talk which portrayed the elder differently was thus both 'nonsense' and 'malicious'. And such talk would undoubtedly have split the congregation into factions, namely, those who remained loyal to the elder and those who chose to follow Diotrephes' lead. Diotrephes, with his self-centred approach, was clearly unconcerned about such a split but the elder's desire for the congregation and for Gaius was that they should experience 'peace'. This peace could clearly only be enjoyed when love and truth be held side by side, so with this benediction we are once again reminded that with the Christian life and the Christian community love and the truth are in fact inseparable.

The word 'friends' used to describe the believers in the elder's own community and those within the church of which Gaius and Diotrephes were a part is very striking. It indicates a personal commitment and shared joy both in relationships and in common endeavour. Those who are friends take a personal interest in one another (note the phrase 'greet by name' in verse 14) and, where possible, they take steps to practically support one another's endeavours. It was precisely such a personal interest and practical support that the elder was seeking within the believing community, not for his own sake, but for the sake of gospel growth, and that is why he wrote to Gaius as he did.

From text to message

As we noted in our discussion of 2 John, there is a real temptation to gloss over the final greeting sections such as 3 John 13-14. Yet having taken some time to think more carefully about this passage and the particular goals that the elder would have had in wording it in the particular way that he did, it becomes clear that it is, indeed, worth teaching from them. In particular, they give the preacher the opportunity to stress the importance of gospel friendship but also to note and underline that such gospel friendships are *gospel* friendships and that they should indeed be maximised so that the gospel may bear fruit and grow all over the world.

Getting the message clear: the theme

- Gospel friendships matter and are worth preserving.
- Gospel friendships should lead to gospel growth.

Getting the message clear: the aim

To encourage true gospel-based, gospel-centred friendships.

A way in

One way in could be to talk about the negative effects that division within a local congregation has upon gospel work. Where Christians are divided the gospel seldom goes forward. The New Testament urges us to pray for peace in society so that the gospel may prosper. In this passage the elder does everything in his power to undermine gossip and the divisions it causes and to urge his readers and ourselves to pursue peace and to work together for the gospel.

Ideas for application

- Gospel friendship is a precious privilege.
- True gospel friendship can only exist around the true gospel.
- Gospel friendship should lead to gospel partnership.

Suggestions for preaching

Sermon

Make it count (3 John 13-14)

1. Introduction
    - The privilege of gospel friendship
    - The purpose of gospel friendship
2. Promoting gospel friendship
    - Relationships matter, so maintain them
    - Truth matters, so quell destructive gossip
    - Partnership matters , so pursue unity and peace
    - People matter, so take time to build gospel relationships
3. Conclusion
    - Make relationships count for the gospel

Suggestions for teaching

Questions to help understand the passage

1. In what way does the phrase 'I have much to write to you' affirm his relationship with Gaius?
2. In what way does this phrase relate to the letter as a whole?
3. Why was the elder anxious to make a personal visit to Gaius and the church?
4. What does the phrase 'face to face' (*lit* mouth to mouth) teach us about the importance of words within Christian relationships?
5. What does the elder want the church to which he is writing to enjoy? Why?

6. What is the possible significance of the word 'soon' in verse 14?

7. Why does the elder refer to the believers in the two communities as 'friends'?

Questions to help apply the passage

1. In what way is the elder's personal and relational approach to the problems he faced an example for us?

2. How important are words for genuine gospel friendship?

3. How can gospel friendships be encouraged within the church?

4. Why are gospel friendships worth building within the church?

5. Why is division within a local church so destructive?

6. How can such divisions be avoided?

FURTHER READING

Raymond E Brown, *The Epistles of John* (New York, USA: Doubleday, 1982)

David Jackman, *The Message of John's Letters* (Leicester, England: IVP, 1988)

Matthew D Jensen, *The Structure and Argument of 1 John* (JSNT 35(1) 54-73) (USA: Sage, 2012)

Matthew D Jensen, *Affirming the Resurrection of the Incarnate Christ* (Cambridge, England: CUP, 2014)

Colin G Kruse, *The Letters of John* (Leicester, England: Apollos, 2000)

I Howard Marshall, *The Epistles of John* (Grand Rapids, USA: Eerdmans, 1978)

John R W Stott, *The Epistles of John* (Leicester, England: IVP)

PT Resources

RESOURCES FOR PREACHERS AND BIBLE TEACHERS

PT Resources, a ministry of The Proclamation Trust, provides a range of multimedia resources for preachers and Bible teachers.

Teach the Bible Series (Christian Focus & PT Resources)
The Teaching the Bible Series, published jointly with Christian Focus Publications, is written by preachers, for preachers, and is specifically geared to the purpose of God's Word – its proclamation as living truth. Books in the series aim to help the reader move beyond simply understanding a text to communicating and applying it.

Current titles include: *Teaching Numbers, Teaching 1 Kings, Teaching Isaiah, Teaching Daniel, Teaching Amos, Teaching Matthew, Teaching Acts, Teaching Romans (in two volumes), Teaching Ephesians, Teaching 1 and 2 Thessalonians, Teaching 1 Timothy, Teaching 2 Timothy, Teaching 1 Peter, Teaching 1, 2, 3 John,* and *Teaching the Christian Hope.*

Practical Preacher series

PT Resources publish a number of books addressing practical issues for preachers. These include *The Priority of Preaching, Bible Delight, Hearing the Spirit* and *The Ministry Medical.*

Online resources

We publish a large number of audio resources online, all of which are free to download. These are searchable through our website by speaker, date, topic and Bible book. The resources include:

- sermon series; examples of great preaching which not only demonstrate faithful principles but which will refresh and encourage the heart of the preacher
- instructions; audio which helps the teacher or preacher understand, open up and teach individual books of the Bible by getting to grips with their central message and purpose
- conference recordings; audio from all our conferences including the annual Evangelical Ministry Assembly. These talks discuss ministry and preaching issues.

An increasing number of resources are also available in video download form.

Online DVD

PT Resources have recently published online our collection of instructional videos by David Jackman. This material has been taught over the past 20 years on our PT Cornhill training course and around the world. It gives step by step instructions on handling each genre of biblical literature. There is also an online workbook. The videos are suitable for preachers and those teaching the Bible in a variety of different contexts. Access to all the videos is free of charge.

The Proclaimer

Visit the Proclaimer blog for regular updates on matters to do with preaching. This is a short, punchy blog refreshed daily which is written by preachers and for preachers. It can be accessed via the PT website or through www.theproclaimer.org.uk.

TEACHING
NUMBERS
ADRIAN REYNOLDS

TEACHING
1 KINGS
BOB FYALL

TEACHING
AMOS
BOB FYALL
SERIES EDITORS: DAVID JACKMAN & ROBIN SYDSERFF

TEACHING
ACTS
Unlocking the book of Acts
for the Bible Teacher
DAVID COOK
SERIES EDITORS: DAVID JACKMAN & ROBIN SYDSERFF

TEACHING
EPHESIANS
From text to message
SIMON AUSTEN
SERIES EDITORS: DAVID JACKMAN & ADRIAN REYNOLDS

TEACHING
1 & 2 THESSALONIANS
From text to message
ANGUS MACLEAY

TEACHING
1 TIMOTHY
From text to message
ANGUS MACLEAY

TEACHING
2 TIMOTHY
From text to message
JONATHAN GRIFFITHS

TEACHING
1 PETER
ANGUS MACLEAY
SERIES EDITORS: DAVID JACKMAN & ROBIN SYDSERFF

Teaching Numbers
Adrian Reynolds
ISBN 978-1-78191-156-3

Teaching 1 Kings
Robert Fyall
ISBN 978-1-78191-605-6

Teaching Isaiah
David Jackman
ISBN 978-1-84550-565-3

Teaching Daniel
Robert Fyall & Robin Sydserff
ISBN 978-1-84550-457-1

Teaching Amos
Robert Fyall
ISBN 978-1-84550-142-6

Teaching Matthew
William Philip & David Jackman
ISBN 978-1-84550-480-9

Teaching Acts
David Cook
ISBN 978-1-84550-255-3

Teaching Romans (volume 1 & 2)
Christopher Ash
ISBN 978-1-84550-455-7 (1) & ISBN 978-1-84550-456-4 (2)

Teaching Ephesians
Simon Austen
ISBN 978-1-84550-684-1

Teaching 1 & 2 Thessalonians
Angus MacLeay
ISBN 978-1-78191-325-3

Teaching 1 Timothy
Angus MacLeay
ISBN 978-1-84550-808-1

Teaching 2 Timothy
Jonathan Griffiths
ISBN 978-1-78191-389-5

Teaching 1 Peter
Angus MacLeay
ISBN 978-1-84550-347-5

Teaching the Christian Hope
David Jackman
ISBN 978-1-85792-518-0

RESOURCES
TEACHING DANIEL
From text to message
ROBERT FYALL & ROBIN SYDSERFF
SERIES EDITORS: DAVID JACKMAN & ADRIAN REYNOLDS

Teaching Daniel
by Robert Fyall & Robin Sydserff

This useful resource, alongside the others in this growing 'Teaching the Bible Series', is for those who have the privilege and joy of teaching or preaching a particular book or theme from the Bible. Whether you're a leader of a small group, preacher or a youth worker, it will help you to communicate the message of Daniel.

Bob Fyall is Senior Tutor in Ministry for the Cornhill Training Course (Scotland). Prior to that he was the Director of Rutherford House, Edinburgh. He is an experienced pastor, preacher and Old Testament scholar.

Robin Sydserff is the minister of Chalmers Church, Edinburgh, having previously served as Director of Ministry for Cornhill.

ISBN: 978-1-84550-457-1

Christian Focus Publications

Our mission statement –

STAYING FAITHFUL

In dependence upon God we seek to impact the world through literature faithful to His infallible Word, the Bible. Our aim is to ensure that the Lord Jesus Christ is presented as the only hope to obtain forgiveness of sin, live a useful life and look forward to heaven with Him.

Our books are published in four imprints:

CHRISTIAN FOCUS

Popular works including biographies, commentaries, basic doc-trine and Christian living.

CHRISTIAN HERITAGE

Books representing some of the best material from the rich heritage of the church.

MENTOR

Books written at a level suitable for Bible College and seminary students, pastors, and other serious readers. The imprint includes commentaries, doctrinal studies, examination of current issues and church history.

CF4•K

Children's books for quality Bible teaching and for all age groups: Sunday school curriculum, puzzle and activity books; personal and family devotional titles, biographies and inspirational stories – because you are never too young to know Jesus!

Christian Focus Publications Ltd,
Geanies House, Fearn, Ross-shire,
IV20 1TW, Scotland, United Kingdom.
www.christianfocus.com